Édouard Glissant

Introduction to a Poetics of Diversity

THE GLISSANT TRANSLATION PROJECT

Édouard Glissant

Introduction to a Poetics of Diversity

translated by
Celia Britton

LIVERPOOL UNIVERSITY PRESS

First published 2020 by
Liverpool University Press
4 Cambridge Street
Liverpool
L69 7ZU

Copyright © 2020 Liverpool University Press

The right of Celia Britton to be identified as the translator of this book has been asserted by her in accordance with the Copyright, Designs and Patents Act 1988.

All rights reserved. No part of this book may be reproduced, stored in a retrieval system, or transmitted, in any form or by any means, electronic, mechanical, photocopying, recording, or otherwise, without the prior written permission of the publisher.

British Library Cataloguing-in-Publication data
A British Library CIP record is available

ISBN 978-1-78962-097-9 cased
ISBN 978-1-78962-129-7 limp

Typeset by Carnegie Book Production, Lancaster

A Timeline for Édouard Glissant

21 September 1928	Édouard Godard is born in the Morne Bezaudin, Martinique.
1935–1939	Primary school, Le Lamentin, Martinique.
1938	Édouard Godard is recognized by his father and becomes Édouard Glissant.
1939–1945	High school.
1944	Glissant founds and directs a journal, *Franc Jeu*.
1946	He leaves Martinique to study ethnology and philosophy (under the philosopher Jean Wahl) in France, at the Université de la Sorbonne.
1948	Publication of Glissant's first poems in the journal *Les temps modernes*, founded by Jean-Paul Sartre and Simone de Beauvoir.
1950	Glissant marries Yvonne Suvélor in Paris. He collaborates with the journal *Présence africaine*.
1952	He receives a Master of Arts in Philosophy. His thesis, under Gaston Bachelard's direction, is entiled *Découverte et conception du monde dans la poésie contemporaine*.
1953	Glissant contributes to the journal *Les Lettres nouvelles*, founded by Maurice Nadeau and Maurice Saillet. *Un champ d'îles* (poems) (Paris, Instance).
1955	*La terre inquiète* (poems) (Paris, éditions du Dragon).
1956	*Les Indes* (poem) (Paris, Le Seuil). *Soleil de la conscience, Poétique I* (essays) (Paris, Le Seuil). Glissant participates in the first congress of black writers and artists in Paris.

1958	*La Lézarde* (novel) (Paris, Le Seuil), which receives the Théophraste Renaudot Prize.
1959	Glissant participates in the second congress of black writers and artists in Rome.
1960	*Le sel noir* (poems) (Paris, Le Seuil). Glissant participates in the FAGA (Front Antillo-Guyanais pour l'Autonomie). He signs the *Manifeste des 121* or *Declaration on the right of insubordination in the Algerian War*.
1961	*Le sang rivé* (poems) (Paris, Le Seuil). Visit to Cuba. Glissant is forbidden to stay in Martinique and assigned to reside in Metropolitan France, as one of the leaders of Antillean separatism.
1964	*Le Quatrième Siècle* (novel) (Paris, Le Seuil). Glissant marries Jacqueline Marie Amélie Hospice in Paris.
1965	Glissant is allowed to return to Martinique.
1967	He creates the *Institut Martiniquais d'Études* (IME), a private school, where many artists and writers will be taught.
1969	*L'Intention poétique, Poétique II* (essays) (Paris, Le Seuil).
1971	Glissant founds the journal *Acoma*, hosted by the Parisian publisher Maspéro.
1975	*Malemort* (novel), (Paris, Le Seuil).
1978	*Monsieur Toussaint* (theatre play) (Paris, Le Seuil).
1979	*Boises* (poems) (éditions Acoma, Martinique).
1980	He defends his PhD in sociology at the Sorbonne University with *summa cum laude*.
1981	*Le Discours antillais* (essay) (Paris, Le Seuil), based on his PhD. *La case du commandeur* (novel) (Paris, Le Seuil).
1982–1988	Director of the *Courrier de l'Unesco* (journal). Glissant meets Sylvie Sémavoine.
1985	*Pays rêvé, pays réel* (poems) (Paris, Le Seuil).
1987	*Mahogany* (novel) (Paris, Le Seuil).
1988	Glissant is named distinguished professor and director of the Center for French and Francophone Studies at Louisiana State University.

1989	Doctor *honoris causa* from the Collège universitaire de Glendon, University of York, Canada. Wins the Puterbaugh Prize and lectures at the University of Oklahoma, Norman, under the aegis of *World Literature Today*.
1990	Glissant moves from Le Seuil to Gallimard. *Poétique de la Relation, Poétique III* (essay) (Paris, Gallimard). *Discours de Glendon* (essay) (Toronto, editions du GREF). Director of the Caribbean Carbet Prize.
1991	*Fastes* (poems) (Toronto, éditions du GREF).
1993	*Tout-Monde* (novel) (Paris, Gallimard). Glissant is named honorary president of the International Parliament of Writers (Paris), of which he was one of the founding members. He is named doctor *honoris causa* by the University of the West Indies, first in Trinidad, then in Jamaica.
1994	He is named distinguished professor at the City University of New York Graduate Center. *Les Grands Chaos* (poems) (Gallimard, Paris).
1996	*Faulkner, Mississippi* (essay) (Paris Stock). *Poèmes complets, Introduction à une poétique du divers* (essay) (Gallimard, Paris).
1997	*Traité du Tout-Monde, Poétique IV* (Paris, Gallimard).
1998	Glissant marries Sylvie Sémavoine in New Jersey.
1999	*Sartorius. Le roman des Batoutos* (novel) (Paris, Gallimard).
2000	*Le Monde incréé, poétrie* (theatre) (Paris, Gallimard), which includes three plays: *Conte de ce que fut la tragédie d'Askia* (1963) *Parabole d'un moulin de la Martinique* (1975) *La Folie Celat* (1987).
2002	Creation of the Édouard Glissant Prize at the University of Paris-VIII (Vincennes) in collaboration with La maison de l'Amérique latine and, later, the Institut du Tout-Monde.
2003	*Ormerod* (novel) (Paris, Gallimard).

2004	Glissant is named doctor *honoris causa* by the University of Bologna, Italy.
2005	*La Cohée du Lamentin, Poétique V* (essay) (Paris, Gallimard).
2006	*Une nouvelle région du monde, Esthétique I* (essay) (Paris, Gallimard).
	Glissant founds the Institut du Tout-Monde in Paris.
	The French president Jacques Chirac asks for his participation in the founding of a National Center of Slavery.
2007	*La Terre magnétique, les errances de Rapa Nui, l'île de Pâques* (with Sylvie Séma) (Paris, Le Seuil).
	Mémoires des esclavages (Paris, Gallimard).
	Quand les murs tombent. L'identité nationale hors-la-loi? (pamphlet) with Patrick Chamoiseau (Paris, Galaade).
2008	*Les Entretiens de Baton Rouge*, interviews with Alexandre Leupin (Paris, Gallimard).
2009	*Philosophie de la Relation*, Paris, Gallimard.
	L'intraitable beauté du monde, adresse à Barack Obama (pamphlet) (Paris, Galaade).
	Manifeste pour les produits de haute nécessité (pamphlet) (Paris, Galaade).
2010	*Philosophie de la Relation, poésie en étendue* (essay), Paris Gallimard.
	10 mai. Mémoires de la traite négrière, de l'esclavage et de leurs abolitions (essay) (Paris, Galaade).
	La terre, le feu, l'Eau et les Vents, une anthologie de la poésie du Tout-Monde (poetry) (Paris, Galaade).
	L'imaginaire des langues, interviews with Lise Gauvin (Paris, Gallimard).
3 February 2011	Death in Paris.
2015	Glissant's archives are declared a national treasure by the French government and transferred to the National French Library (BNF).

Timeline established with the help of Professors Jean-Pierre Sainton and Raphaël Lauro.

Preface

Introduction to a Poetics of Diversity is, in many ways, an anomalous text in the wider context of Edouard Glissant's *oeuvre*. Unlike a number of his other non-fictional prose writings, it was not associated with the two strands entitled *esthétique* (aesthetics) and *poétique* (poetics) under which works such as *Soleil de Conscience* (Sun of Consciousness; 1956) and *L'Intention poétique* (Poetic Intention, 1969) were retrospectively assembled, and for which others such as *Poétique de la Relation* (Poetics of Relation, 1990) were written directly. In that sense, *Introduction* has similarities with several other books – including *Le Discours antillais* (Caribbean Discourse, 1981) and *Faulkner Mississippi* (1996) – that represent punctual critical interventions and function as a result as works that prove to be *sui generis*.

Introduction belongs nevertheless to a remarkably rich corpus of critical and theoretical writings, beginning with *Poétique de la Relation* in 1990, associated with the final two decades of Glissant's career. During that late period, only one of the author's eight fictional works was published, a final novel *Ormerod* in 2003, as he focused instead on a series of seventeen essays, interviews, manifestos and anthologies that reflected the culmination of a lifetime's reflection on questions of culture, language, memory, history and the creation of knowledge in the Caribbean and beyond.

Before 1990, Glissant had been known in particular for his fiction and poetry, with his widely celebrated works including the Renaudot-winning *La Lézarde* (The Ripening, 1958). Three other very different texts written in this earlier period and gathered loosely under the generic label of the essay – *Soleil de Conscience*, *L'Intention poétique* and *Le Discours antillais* – contain in embryo the key strands of the author's thinking on poetics, diversity and relation, but it was in works published in the final decade of the twentieth century and the opening one of the twenty-first that this intellectual contribution would be broadened, deepened and amplified, reaching wider audiences on both sides of the Atlantic and elsewhere. This flourishing of activity can be mapped closely onto a major shift in Glissant's life and career. Having returned in 1965 to Martinique, where he edited the journal *Acoma* and directed the Institut martiniquais d'études (activity that fed into the collection of essays in *Le Discours antillais*), he spent much of the 1980s in Paris as editor of the *Courrier de l'Unesco* before moving to Louisiana State University as Distinguished Professor in 1988. In 1994, he moved to his final post of Professor of French Literature in the Graduate Center at City University of New York. This period in the USA was one of intense activity, including a collaboration with Jacques Derrida, Salman Rushdie and Pierre Bourdieu in the establishment of the International Parliament of Writers in 1993. At the same time, his international visibility grew, with a number of colloquia devoted to his work and nominations for the Nobel Prize for Literature.

Publication of the *Introduction* – initially in Quebec in 1995, and the following year with Gallimard in Paris (to whom, with *Poétique de la Relation*, the author had switched from Seuil in 1990) – coincided with Glissant's move to the City University of New York (CUNY). The book appeared simultaneously with the deeply personal reflection on the American South in *Faulkner Mississippi*. *Introduction* was moreover sandwiched between the two texts – the diptych formed by the novel *Tout-Monde* (Whole-World, 1993) and the *Traité du Tout-Monde* (Treatise of the Whole-World, 1997) – that established Glissant as a key thinker of globalization. The present text is very different from these other works that form its immediate context. Glissant was a remarkably versatile author, working throughout his career across genres, notably poetry, theatre, fiction, manifestos and the essay. In an interview with Lise Gauvin from the volume *L'Imaginaire des langues* that is included in the current book, Glissant describes the essay as having 'something of poetic writing when it is a tool of discovery, when its purpose is to delve into a subject' (Rethinking Utopia, p. 109). *Introduction* broadly reflects these hallmarks and certainly falls into this generic category, although it is important to note that, for the Martinican author, essayistic writing allowed a flexibility of approaches that ranged from the poetic overtones of *Soleil de Conscience* to the social science emphases of certain chapters in *Le Discours antillais*. In many of Glissant's essays, the conceptual complexity of their content is reflected in a syntactic and lexical density that prove challenging to the reader and translator. The chapters of *Introduction* are 'intertwined', but the book is, as the title suggests, of a different order, playing a more didactic and even pedagogical role that reflects the work's beginnings as a series of lectures delivered in Arles, Perpignan, Bologna and Parma, and reminding us above all of Glissant's relatively recent role as a university teacher in the

USA. As such, it is arguably one of the most accessible of the author's texts, written with the wider understanding of his work as a key aim. It is as a result an ideal starting point for those wanting an initial overview of the concepts and ideas underpinning Glissantian thought.

Given the circumstances of the book's production, rooted in the oral performance of the lecture, the presence in *Introduction* of other voices is essential to a reading of the work and to grasping its fundamentally dialogic nature. First, there are those audience members (Joël Desrosiers, Gaston Miron, Pierre Nepveu and others) with whom Glissant interacts after each intervention and the transcript of their exchanges; secondly, there are the interviews with Lise Gauvin, writer and critic from Quebec and one of Glissant's most sensitive readers; thirdly, there is a need to understand the niche in which the book was the produced and the ways in which Glissant responds in his work to contemporary social challenges, notably the ethnic conflicts and wars of independence that tore up the former Yugoslavia between 1991 and 2001, or the continued attempts of Haitian boatpeople to access the USA – and posits in reaction to these pressing issues the forms of 'multicultural citizenship based on the diversity of cultures and the equality of rights' (Culture and Identity, p. 41) that would characterize many of his political interventions in the final decade of his life; and fourthly, there are the authors who serve as intertextual interlocutors in the work itself. It is via this final type of exchange that the reader is offered a glimpse into the writer's working methods and reminded that many of Glissant's ideas – as is evidenced by collections of essays such as *L'Intention poétique* and *Poétique de la Relation* – emerged from sustained dialogues with other authors and thinkers. In *Introduction*, there are traces of this process in references to conversations with Alejo Carpentier; the impact of Deleuze and Guattari's *Mille plateaux* and the rhizomatic thinking underpinning that work is also made amply clear; the role of Saint-John Perse – the poet born Alexis Leger in Guadeloupe – is evident; but it is the Breton poet, naval officer and theorist of the exotic Victor Segalen (1878–1919) who has the greatest presence in the book.

Most importantly in this regard, Glissant makes it clear in the brief preface to *Introduction* that his title was chosen 'in homage to Victor Segalen' (p. 1). The 'poetics of diversity' to which the book serves a primer was central also to the work of the earlier Franco-Breton writer, active in the first two decades of the twentieth century until his premature death in 1919. Glissant's interest in Segalen dated back to the 1950s, when he first discovered the author's work while a student in Paris. This early encounter led to a lifelong dialogue. Segalen features as a point of reference throughout Glissant's writing, and he is one of the writers included in one of his final works, *La Terre le feu l'eau et les vents: une anthologie de la poésie du Tout-monde* (Earth, Fire and Water: Anthology of the Poetry of The Whole-World, 2010), in which Glissant gathered texts by the authors who had had a major influence on his thinking. Although there are occasional references to the writer of the *Essai sur l'exotisme: une esthétique du Divers* (Essay on Exoticism: An Aesthetics of Diversity) throughout *Introduction*, it is in the exchanges following the chapter on culture and identity that its author provides the only sustained commentary on a writer whose work, he states, 'produces, invents, imagines and constructs a system of exoticist thought that combats all exoticism and all colonization' (p. 49). The distinction between, on the one hand, the later twentieth-century Martinican writer and thinker and, on the other, an early twentieth-century 'military doctor who worked on an escort vessel', is underlined. Glissant detects in his interlocutor, however, a 'revolutionary poet' and concludes with a statement of the poet's importance in the elaboration of his work: 'Honour and respect to Segalen. He was the first to ask the question of the world's diversity, to fight against exoticism as a complacent form of colonization; and he was a doctor of a military ship.'

Segalen's place in the elaboration of Glissant's thought is clear throughout the book, as the former's notions of 'diversity' and 'exoticism' enter into dialogue with the latter's 'relation', as Segalenian entropy encounters Glissantian chaos, and as Glissant underlines the importance, as did Segalen himself, of maintaining firm groundings associated with the opacity or impenetrability of cultures: 'If one enters the diversity of the world,' notes Glissant in response to a question to Lise Gauvin, 'having renounced one's own identity, one gets lost in a sort of confusion' (The Writer and the Breath of Place, p. 89). Although *Introduction* does not engage in detail with Segalen's work (such close analysis is afforded in other works, most notably *L'Intention poétique*), the reading of texts such as *Stèles* and the *Essai sur l'exotisme* is evident throughout the current work as we navigate Glissant's thinking on questions of identity and in particular the dynamics associating self with other: 'how can one be oneself without closing oneself off to the other, and how can one open oneself to the other without losing oneself?' (Creolizations in the Caribbean and the Americas, p. 11). At the same time, the reflections on translation, multilingualism and writing in the 'presence of all the world's languages' reveal a poetic sensitivity dependent on an inability to write monolingually that Glissant had developed following his encounter with Segalen's work in the 1950s.

Introduction contains a condensed account of Glissant's extensive thinking on the place of his native Caribbean in the frames of the Americas and the wider Atlantic. Published in the final decade of the twentieth century, the book explores a wider *fin-de-siècle* world undergoing a process of creolization and 'archipelagization'. It bears witness in the process to the emergence of unforeseeable linguistic and social formations. In the text that follows Glissant provides a lucid explanation of the influential concepts he has bequeathed to those seeking to make sense of the entangled, interrelated, interdependent cultures of a globalized world: 'relation', 'trace', 'wandering', the 'right to opacity'… Moving beyond 'single root-identities' to reveal 'rhizome-identities', Glissant explores the tensions between the atavistic and the composite, challenging in the process the populist rhetorics of cultural purity, of ethnolinguistic nationalism, and of ideological monolingualism, which have received sudden legitimation in the opening decades of the twenty-first century. *Introduction to a Poetics of Diversity* is an eloquent, spontaneous, dynamic reminder of the importance of Edouard Glissant's thinking as we seek to navigate the hypercontemporary whilst locating this troubled current moment in a historical frame.

Charles Forsdick

Introduction to a Poetics of Diversity
Contents

This book reproduces the text of *Introduction à une poétique du divers* and also four further interviews from *L'Imaginaire des langues*. It consists of four lectures and six interviews.

Lectures

1. Creolizations in the Caribbean and the Americas	3
2. Languages and *langages*	19
3. Culture and Identity	37
4. The Chaos-world: Towards an Aesthetic of Relation	53

Interviews

5. The Imagination of Languages	75
6. The Writer and the Breath of Place	87
7. Watching Out for the World	101
8. Rethinking Utopia	109
9. On Beauty as Complicity	117
10. Movements of Languages and Territories of the Novel	127

Lectures

The text of these four lectures, whose title I have chosen in homage to Victor Segalen, probably suffers from an excess of 'theory', where I should have addressed the Diverse and the intertwinings of the 'Whole-World'* through a wave of poetic approaches, through descriptions of landscapes and situations, through a resonant play of harmonies and disharmonies that would have expressed our common 'being-in-the-world'. But in this case the rule is to try to say as much as possible in the allotted time and to focus, if not on what is clearest, then at least on what is most immediately convincing.

This is a work composed in a single continuous period of time, where the spoken word almost always prevails over the reservations of writing and where the 'I' is excessively prominent, all the more so in that the interviews that follow the lectures inevitably reinforce the sense of commitment and taking up of positions. I hope that the dominant feeling after reading it will be of a search, perhaps anxious or wandering, rather than of a system closed in on itself.

My thanks go to Jean-Claude Castelain, Joël Desrosiers, Lise Gauvin, Jean-Claude Gémar, Robert Melançon, Gaston Miron, Pierre Nepveu, among others, who have accompanied me on this path. And also to Martin Robitaille who undertook the transcription of the whole text.

É. G.

---

* Glissant's *Traité du Tout-monde* (Paris: Editions Gallimard, 1997) discusses the concept of the 'Whole-World', which it defines as 'our universe as it changes and persists through its exchanges and, at the same time, the 'vision' that we have of it' (p. 176, my translation).

Creolizations in the Caribbean and the Americas*

The topic of these four lectures will appear complex and erratic, and in the course of my expositions I will probably revisit themes, which will be intertwined and modified: that is my way of working.

My first approach to what has been called the Americas – the first experience I had of them – was of the landscape, even before becoming aware of the collective or private human dramas that had accumulated within it. The American landscape – and I am referring to the countries of the Americas, in the plural – has always struck me as very different from what I have been able to learn of European landscapes, for instance. These have always seemed to me to make up a tightly regulated ensemble, with a strict timetable, connected to a kind of ritualized rhythm of the seasons. Every time I come back to the Americas, whether to an island like Martinique, the country of my birth, or the American continent, I am struck by the openness of this landscape. I call it 'irrué' – a word I have invented, of course – implying irruption and rush [*ruade*], also eruption, perhaps a lot of the real and a lot of the unreal [*irréel*]. And I feel as though when I stand on the heights of Sainte-Marie on the Bezaudin hill, my birthplace, and see the espaliered crops, almost vertical in these higher reaches of Bezaudin and another hill called Pérou, and yet another called Reculée, I have the same sensation as in a much bigger, far more spacious landscape: that of Chávin in Peru. Chávin is the cradle of pre-Inca agriculture where I have seen these same espaliered crops, where one wonders how the peasant working there does not fall off the thirty-centimetre-wide path on which he places his feet.

---

* Lecture given at the Assises Internationales de la traduction, Arles, 1994.

In these spaces, the eye cannot master the ruses and subtleties of perspective; one's gaze does not distinguish the vertical and the horizontal but just takes in a rocky piling up of the real.

This American landscape that one finds in a small island or on the continent seems to me always equally 'irrué'. And that is probably the source of a feeling I have always had, of a sort of unity-diversity between on the one hand the Caribbean countries and, on the other, all those that make up the American continent. In this sense, the Caribbean has also always seemed to be a kind of preface to the continent. In the sixteenth and seventeenth centuries, the Caribbean Sea was called the Sea of Peru, even though Peru is on the other side of the continent and there is no possible connection between them. The sea was a kind of introduction to the continent, a kind of link between what one must leave behind and what one must endeavour to get to know.

The Caribbean was the site of the first landing of the transported slaves, transported Africans – after which they were sent either to North America, or Brazil, or the islands of the region. These Caribbean countries have always seemed to me, not exemplary – I distrust the notion of exemplarity – but significant, in the sense of signifying the American continent as a whole. And yet, these are countries that were ignored for a long time – apart from Haiti, the first black republic in the history of the world, and Cuba and the Cuban revolution. What I would like to do today is not to glorify them, but to show that they point to something that is happening in the Americas as a whole, with many shocks and disruptions, and that I will attempt to study with you.

I will start by defining what I, among others, take to be the primary characteristic of the Americas: that is, the division that one can make – along with researchers such as Darcy Ribeiro in Brazil and Emmanuel Bonfil Batalla in Mexico or Rex Nettleford in Jamaica – into three kinds of America. There is the America of the peoples who have borne witness, those who have always been there, that is defined as *meso-America*; the America of those who arrived from Europe and who have preserved on the new continent the customs and traditions of their birth countries, that one could call *Euro-America* and which of course includes Quebec, Canada, the United States and a (cultural) part of Chile and Argentina; and the America that one could call *neo-America* and that is the America of creolization. This is made up of the Caribbean, the north-east of Brazil, the Guyanas and Curaçao, the south of the United States, the Caribbean coast of Venezuela and Columbia, and a large part of central America and Mexico.

This division does not involve frontiers; these three Americas are imbricated in one another. *Meso-America* exists in Quebec and Canada as well as the United States. A country like Venezuela or Columbia includes a Caribbean part and an Andean part, that is, a *neo-America* and a *meso-America*. In these continents and these islands, the clashes and conflicts between these three kinds of America have multiplied. But also, the predominant feature of this relationship is that *neo-America*, i.e. the America of creolization, while it continues to borrow from *meso-America* and *Euro-America*, is tending more and more to influence these other two forms of the American division. And what is interesting in the phenomenon of creolization, the phenomenon that constitutes *neo-America*, is that the population that makes up *neo-America* is very specific. Here Africa dominates.

One could say that there have been roughly three kinds of people contributing to the population of the Americas. The 'armed migrant', who disembarks from the *Mayflower* or sails up the Saint Lawrence River. He comes with his boats, his weapons, etc., and is the 'founding migrant'. Then there is the 'family migrant', the domestic migrant, who comes with his tin trunk, his oven, his saucepans and his family photos, and settles in large areas of North and South America. And finally there is what I call the 'naked migrant' – that is, the migrant who has been forcibly transported into the continent and forms the basis of the population of that kind of fundamental circularity that for me the Caribbean represents. This term 'circularity' is important because the process is indeed a sort of radiation outwards, a spiralling, quite different from the shooting upwards that characterizes all colonizations.

I always say that the Caribbean Sea differs from the Mediterranean in so far as it is an open sea, a sea that diffracts, while the Mediterranean is a sea that concentrates. Civilizations and the great monotheistic religions have grown up around the Mediterranean basin because this sea has the power, even through crises, wars and conflicts, to bend men's thoughts towards ideas of sameness and unity. Whereas the Caribbean Sea is a sea that diffracts, and so leads us into the turmoil of diversity. It is not only a sea of transit and passage, but also of encounters and involvements. What has been happening in the Caribbean for the last three centuries is literally this: a coming together of cultural elements from absolutely diverse horizons, which become truly creolized, which really interlink and mix with one another to produce something absolutely unforeseeable, absolutely new: Creole reality. *Neo-America* – whether in Brazil, on the Caribbean coasts, in the islands or in the south of the United

States – experiences the reality of creolization against a background of slavery, oppression, dispossession by the various systems of slavery, whose abolition extends over a long period of time (roughly from 1830 to 1868); and through these dispossessions, these oppressions and these crimes, achieves a true conversion of 'Being'.*

It is this conversion of Being that I want to study with you in the course of these four lectures. My argument will be the following: the creolization that is happening in neo-America, and the creolization that is spreading to the other Americas, is the same as that which is operating in the world as a whole. The argument that I will put before you is that *the world is creolizing*: that is, the world's cultures today, brought into contact with each other at lightning speed, in an absolutely conscious manner, change through exchange with each other, by way of inexorable clashes, pitiless wars, but also of advances in consciousness and hope, which enable us to claim – without being utopian, or rather, by embracing utopianism – that today's human communities are engaging in the difficult process of giving up something to which they have obstinately clung for a long time: that is, the conviction that the identity of a being is valid and recognizable only if it excludes the identity of all other possible beings. And it is this painful mutation in human thought that I would like to explore with you.

What is creolization? I have suggested that there are three kinds of settlement, and that it is settlement by transportation from Africa that has caused the most suffering and unhappiness in the Americas – if one does not count the extermination of the Amerindian peoples in the north and the south of the continent; and of course one must count this. There is today a fourth, internal, form of population movement: that of the Haitian and Cuban boat people. This is a crucial factor in the evolution of American societies. But if we examine the three historical forms of settlement, we see that while the people migrating from Europe, such as the Scots, Irish, Italians, Germans, French, etc., arrive together with their songs, their family traditions, their tools, the image of their god, etc., the Africans arrive stripped of everything, of every possibility, and even of their language. For the hold of the slave ship is the place and the time where the African languages disappear, because people who spoke the same language were never put on the same slave ship or indeed the same plantation. Their

---

* Where Glissant distinguishes in the phenomenological sense between 'l'être' and 'l'étant' I have translated these terms as 'Being' and 'being' respectively.

being found itself denuded of all kinds of elements of its daily life, and above all of its language.

What happens to this migrant? He reconstructs, on the basis of *traces*, a language and forms of art that one could say are valid for everyone. While, for example, in an ethnic community on the American continent, people have kept alive the memory of the songs of burial, of weddings, baptism, joy or pain from the old country and have been singing them for a hundred years or more on the various occasions of family life, the deported African has not had the opportunity of preserving these kinds of specific inheritances. But he has made something new on the basis of the only memories, that is to say the only *trace* thoughts, that he had left: he has created on the one hand the Creole languages and, on the other, art forms that are valid for everyone, such as the music of jazz, which has been reconstituted with the help of newly adopted instruments but on the basis of fundamental African rhythms. Although this neo-American does not sing African songs from two or three centuries ago, he re-establishes in the Caribbean, Brazil and North America, through 'trace thought', art forms that he offers as valid for all peoples. Trace thought seems to me to be a new dimension that in the current state of the world we must set in opposition to what I call 'systematic thought' or systems of thought. Systematic thought and systems of thought were prodigiously fruitful and prodigiously dominant and prodigiously deadly. Trace thought is that which today most validly opposes the false universality of systematic thought.

The phenomena of creolization are important because they enable us to put into practice a new approach to the spiritual dimension of humanity. An approach that involves a reorganization of the mental landscape of these human communities today. For creolization presupposes that the cultural elements brought together must necessarily be 'of equivalent value' for this creolization to be truly realized. That is to say that if some of the cultural elements brought together are seen as inferior to others, creolization does not really happen. It happens, but in a bastardized and unjust fashion. In creolized countries such as the Caribbean or Brazil, where the cultural elements have been put in place by the mode of settlement that was the transportation of Africans, the African and black cultural constituents have routinely been treated as inferior. Creolization still happens in these conditions, but it leaves a bitter, uncontrollable residue. And almost everywhere in neo-America the balance between the elements brought together has had to be reset, primarily by revalorization of the African heritage, such as the movement of Haitian indigenism, or the Harlem Renaissance, or Negritude – Damas's and Césaire's poetics of Negritude meeting up with Senghor's theory of Negritude. The active creolization going on within the belly of the plantation – that most unjust and sinister world – is nevertheless *creating* itself, but it leaves the 'Being' struggling. Because the 'Being' is destabilized by its inner diminution, which it feigns to see as such, the diminution, for example, of its properly African value. This is also happening in the Antilles and the Caribbean for other ethnic groups. Among these the Hindu element, when after 1848 the countries of the Caribbean were partially populated by Indian migrants who were promised that they would find work there, but who were treated purely and simply as slaves. There too there has been a discrediting of the values coming from India, and it has taken a long time for people to recognize, as they do today, that communities of Indian descent form an important part of the phenomenon of creolization in the Caribbean. In Trinidad, the population is split more or less equally between the Indian and the African communities.

Creolization requires the heterogenous elements put into relation to 'intervalorize' themselves: that is to say, there must be no degradation or diminution of the being, either from outside or within, in this contact and intermixing. And why creolization rather than hybridity ['métissage']? Because creolization is unforeseeable, whereas one can calculate in advance the effects of hybridity. The effects of a hybridization of plants through grafting or of animals through crossbreeding can be calculated; one can predict that mixing red beans and white beans by grafting will produce a certain result after one generation, a different result after another generation. But creolization is hybridity with an added value, namely unforeseeability. Thus it was completely unpredictable that 'trace thoughts' would lead the populations of the Americas towards the creation of such new languages or art forms. Unlike hybridity, creolization works with the unforeseeable; it creates across the Americas completely unexpected cultural and linguistic microclimates, places where the repercussions of languages on each other, of cultures on each other, are sudden and surprising. In Louisiana for instance, the creation of zydeco music imports into traditional Cajun music the rhythms and powers of jazz and even rock. In Louisiana there are *Black Indians*, that is, tribes born of a mixture of escaped black slaves and Indians. In New Orleans I have watched the procession of *Black Indian* ethnicities, and seen in them something absolutely unforeseeable, which goes beyond the simple fact of hybridity. These cultural and linguistic microclimates that are created by creolization in the Americas are crucial because they are the actual signs of what is really happening in the world. And what is really happening in the world, is that micro- and macroclimates of cultural and linguistic interpenetration are being created. And when this cultural and linguistic interpenetration is very strong, the old demons of purity and anti-hybridity react against it, and set on fire these infernal flashpoints that we see burning on the surface of the world.

Why choose the term creolization to designate all these shocks, harmonies, distortions, retreats, repulsions and attractions between elements of culture? I have already said why the word 'hybridity' must be rejected here. The word 'creolization' of course derives from the term 'Creole' and the reality of the Creole languages. And what is a Creole language? It is a composite language, emerging from contact between entirely heterogeneous linguistic elements. The francophone languages of the Caribbean were born from the bringing together of seventeenth-century Breton and Norman dialects with a syntax whose origin we do not really know, but which we can guess is a kind of synthesis of the languages of black sub-Saharan Western Africa. In other words, the vocabulary of the Norman dialect has nothing to do with this syntax, which is perhaps a 'syntactic synthesis' of these African languages. The combination of the two moreover begins, whatever one may say to the contrary, as merely a pidgin, because its function is to regulate the problems of labour in the Caribbean islands. But the combination is unforeseeable. It was absolutely unforeseeable that in two centuries an enslaved community should have produced a language on the basis of such heterogeneous elements. I define a Creole language as a language whose constitutive elements are mutually heterogeneous. I do not, for instance, define as Creole the splendid language of the Jamaican dub poets, like Michael Smith and Linton Kwesi Johnson or Edward Kamau Brathwaite. This is said to be a Jamaican Creole – perhaps one should invent a new word – but I do not call it a Creole because what it is, is the brilliant and aggressive deformation of *one* language, the English language, from within that language, by subversive users of that language. I am not setting up any hierarchy here. Is it a pidgin? But 'pidgin' is so negative and pejorative that one cannot apply it to such a language. My Jamaican friends have told me that this language cannot be a pidgin, that it is a Creole. I do not believe that it is a Creole and we must find another term because a Creole is at least double, that is, it has at least two constitutive elements, whether it is the criolo of Cape Verde, the crio of Senegal, the papiamento of Curaçao, or indeed the Martiniquan, Haitian, Guadeloupean, Réunion, St Lucian or Dominican Creoles. Creoles are created by the clash, the consumption, the reciprocal consumption of linguistic elements that were originally completely heterogeneous to each other, producing an unforeseeable result. A Creole is therefore not the result of that superb operation that the Jamaican poets deliberately and committedly carry out on the English language; nor is it a pidgin or a dialect. It is something new, that we are beginning to become aware of, but of which we cannot say if it is an original phenomenon, since when we investigate rationally the origins of all languages, including French, we realize (or we sense) that almost every language is at its origins a Creole language.

As far as the francophone Creoles of the Caribbean and the Indian Ocean are concerned, my hypotheses are the following:

The French, Breton and Norman dialects were sufficiently unstable to allow the emergence of the Creole phenomenon (linguistic creolization), whereas Spanish and English, already strongly 'organic' and established, resisted creolization almost everywhere.

It is probable that linguistic creolization operates more effectively on small and clearly delimited territories: islands, whether or not these are organized into archipelagos (Caribbean, Indian Ocean, Cape Verde). In a sense, laboratories. These hypotheses do not credit the French language with creolization, as some people have supposed or claimed that I suppose.

For these reasons I believe that the term creolization applies to the world today, that is, the situation in which a 'totality earth', finally realized, means that within this totality (where there is no longer any 'organic' authority and everything is an archipelago), the most distant and most heterogeneous elements possible can be put into relation with each other. This produces unforeseeable results.

This perception of what is happening in the world is based on the distinction, which we now have to make, between two generic forms of culture. Forms that I will call atavistic, that were creolized a very long time ago, and whose nature we will study later; and forms that I will call composite, where creolization is happening practically before our very eyes. The countries of the Caribbean and of that expanding circularity that I have mentioned are examples of these composite cultures. One can see that the composite cultures are in the process of becoming atavistic, in other words of claiming a kind of permanence, of temporal respectability, that would seem to be necessary for any culture to be sure of itself and have the confidence to assert itself. Equally, the atavistic cultures are tending to creolize, that is to question, or to defend often dramatically

– see Yugoslavia, Lebanon, etc. – the status of identity as a single root. Because in fact that is what is at stake here: a sublime and deadly idea that the peoples of Europe and Western cultures have transported around the world, i.e. that every identity is a *root-identity* exclusive of all others. This view of identity is opposed to the idea, 'real' today in composite cultures, of identity as factor and result of a creolization: that is, of identity as rhizome, identity no longer a single root, but a root reaching out to other roots. As soon as this is formulated it raises worrying problems, because if we talk about a root-identity reaching out towards other roots, we sense a threat of dilution: we are still functioning according to the old model, and I feel as though if I reach out to contact the other then I am no longer myself, and if I am no longer myself then I am lost! In the panorama of the world today, a major question is: how can one be oneself without closing oneself off to the other, and how can one open oneself to the other without losing oneself? This is the question posed and illustrated by the composite cultures in the world of the Americas. Where is the point of contact between these composite cultures that are moving towards atavism and these atavistic cultures that are beginning to creolize?

This question absolutely must be discussed if we wish, via a detour, to escape the deadly, bloody oppositions that now motivate and aggravate the disorder of the world. Must we give up the spirituality, the mentality and the imagination* that derive from the conception of identity as a single root that kills everything around it, to enter into the *difficult* constitution of a *relational* identity, an identity that involves an opening up to the other, without risk of dilution? If we do not ask ourselves this kind of question, it seems to me that we are not in symbiosis, not in relation, with the real situation of the world, of what is happening in the world. And I think that only a poetics of Relation, that is, an imagination, will allow us to 'understand' these phases and these implications of peoples' situations in the world today, and will perhaps give us a means of trying to escape the imprisonment to which we are reduced. I think there are places in the world where this kind of challenge and this kind of impossible change are playing out, for example in South Africa. One of the main aims of the

---

* 'l'imaginaire'. In English, 'the imaginary' is associated primarily with its use in the work of Lacan and Althusser, where it has a rather different meaning. I have therefore preferred to translate 'l'imaginaire' here as 'imagination', which should be understood not as the faculty of imagining but as a kind of distinctive repertoire of images that orientate one's thinking, in the sense in which we speak of 'the Romantic imagination', 'the Puritan imagination', etc.

ANC and Nelson Mandela is of course to solve the problems of economic survival for that whole section of the population that for so long has been kept in poverty and slavery by the apartheid regime. But I think there is also something else at stake that involves the twenty-first century: if the ANC and Nelson Mandela are not able to get the Zulus, the blacks, the coloureds, the Indians and the whites to live together in South Africa, then something of our twenty-first century, our future, the future of the humanities that we represent, will be visibly threatened and visibly lost. At the end of his autobiography, Nelson Mandela poses this question, and more or less in these terms: 'The whole distance that I have travelled to get here [from 1912 to 1994], all these struggles, are as nothing compared to what we still have to do, because what we still have to do is the most important thing, and that is to get all these communities to live together'.*
This is what I mean by leaving behind the single root-identity and entering into the truth of the creolization of the world. I think that we must in future move towards trace thought, towards a non-system of thought that will not be dominating, nor systematic, nor imposing, but will perhaps be a non-system of thought – intuitive, fragile, ambiguous –which will be best suited to the extraordinary complexity, the extraordinary dimension of multiplicity of the world in which we live. Traversed and supported by the trace, the landscape ceases to be just a suitable décor and becomes a character in the *drama* of Relation. It is no longer the passive envelope of the all-powerful Narrative, but the changing and enduring dimension of all change and all exchange. This imagination of a trace thought is an integral part of us when we live a poetics of Relation in the world today.

Diversity extends to include all the unexpected emergences, minorities that yesterday were still unknown and crushed by a monolithic thought-system, fractal manifestations of sensibilities that reshape and rearrange themselves in new ways.

All possibilities and all contradictions are inscribed in this diversity of the world. In Martinique for example, one cannot but be aware of a kind of participation in the vibrancy of the Caribbean, a growing vibrancy which is at last bringing together the hispanophone, anglophone, francophone and other (creolophone) Caribbeans – while at the same time, in the same country of Martinique, we witness a flood of fashions (in music, food, clothing) that subject the Martiniquans passively to 'planetary' influxes that are certainly alienating, because they are adopted uncritically.

---

* Nelson Mandela, *Long Walk to Freedom* [1994], (London: Abacus, 2002), vol. 2, p. 235.

QUESTIONS

Robert Melançon. I will start with a point of detail: I noted rather hurriedly the definition you gave of creolization, and I will try to repeat it correctly and not to misquote you: 'The most distant heterogeneous elements are brought together and produce an unforeseeable result'. It seems to me that the force and the unforeseeability of the result are due to the distance between the elements that are brought together. It seems to me that this irresistibly calls to mind Breton's and Reverdy's definition of the poetic image, which brings together two elements as distant as possible from each other, and it is from the shock of this distance that something unforeseeable is born, something that we call the image. So my first question is: do you agree with this comparison?

É.G. Absolutely. It would confirm that the poetic act is one element of knowledge of the real.

R.M. My second question is much broader. You have very convincingly described a process of world creolization that is happening now, and you have mentioned, rapidly but enough for us to understand you, earlier creolizations, such as that of the ancient world by the arrival of Christianity and of these new peoples who were called 'barbarians'. And therefore, could one not redefine creolization as a state of turbulence of systems which are brought together, and is one not therefore led to think that after a fairly long period of turbulence there will inevitably be a stasis? You said yourself that all languages, if one digs into their roots a little, were originally Creoles. Won't the world creolization happening today, when the earth is finally one, lead to a state of unification which would completely stop the movement, because there would no longer be any external elements, foreign elements?

É.G. Regarding your first point, I agree entirely on the definition of the poetic image, especially by Reverdy – I think he got closer to it than Breton did.
As for the phenomenon of creolization: an important dimension of contemporary creolization is its lightning speed and its self-awareness. Cultural contacts have always taken place, but they were stretched out over such long periods of time that they did not attain consciousness. That is, a Gallo-Roman of the eighth century – they still existed then – was not

conscious that he was a 'combination' of Gaul and of Rome. He believed that he was forever a Roman citizen. The cultural outcome had not attained consciousness because it was taken for granted. The fantastic thing about modern creolization is that, with its lightning speed, it enters into our consciousness. When I see on television an earthquake in a country somewhere, with lightning speed I not only become aware of the earthquake, but I am almost immersed in the language of the people who have suffered this earthquake, their way of life, what they have lost, etc. I immediately think of the earthquake that *will come* to my own country. I am immersed in all this, and that is why I often say that the contemporary writer, the modern writer, is not monolingual, even if he knows only one language, because he writes in the presence of all the world's languages. Now, would this process – for creolization is a process – come to a final state, a final phase? I do not think so, because it is consciousness that reactivates the process and it is non-science, non-knowledge, that would stabilize it into a defined identity. I believe that we have arrived at a moment in the life of human communities in which the human being is beginning to accept the idea that he is himself perpetually in process, that he is not Being, but a being, and that like all beings, he changes. And I think that this is one of the major intellectual, spiritual and mental permutations of our age, which means that we are all afraid. We are all afraid of this idea that one day we are going to admit that we are not an absolute entity, but a changing being. And I believe that this notion of consciousness and lightning speed means that in future we will not arrive at a new stasis, a new phase of fixity, so to speak. Unless this totality-earth, finally realized, comes up against another absolute. For example if we come into contact with extra-terrestrials. That would then be the other absolute that would oppose the identity of the earth. And at that moment the process does indeed run the risk of becoming fixed in a new single-identity earth which would be opposed to the other absolute, absolutely foreign. But apart from that eventuality, I do not believe that creolization can stop and become fixed.

Q. In my opinion, Creole is a fairly 'local' reality, and even if the global process you describe is identical, one cannot extrapolate from the particular situation of Creole to the situation of the world.

É.G. I do not completely agree. Languages that today are local are indeed called Creoles, but as I have said, I believe that all languages were originally Creoles. It's just that the speakers of those languages, as soon as they were aware of it, wanted their language to no longer be a Creole but to be specific. The dream of every human community is that its language was given to them by a god, in other words that its language is the language of an exclusive identity. A year ago I was in a discussion with two Japanese novelists at Strasbourg, who told me: 'There is a great debate in Japan, with a lot at stake. The fascists claim that the Japanese language is pure, given to them by a god. And we for our part claim that the Japanese language is a Creole language. And that there have been borrowings' (they even speak of Basque, of Indonesian and Korean languages). There is a lot at stake here. One of the writers of this same group, who died two years ago, wrote a book which has not yet been translated into French, called *Creolisms*. In other words the phenomenon I am describing is not in any way local: it is a far more general issue. And if I choose the term creolization, I am not referring to my home town or the Antilles or the Caribbean. It is because nothing else gives a better idea of what is happening in the world than this unforeseeable coming together of heterogeneous elements.

This question is one which in the present time is being asked all over the world, because *it is* the situation of the world. When I say 'creolization', I am not referring at all to the Creole language, I am referring to the *phenomenon* that has structured the Creole languages, which is not the same thing.

Q. Do you see in this process of creolization the possibility of a 'danger', in so far as it could lead to a certain relativization of the land of one's birth?

É.G. There is an intense rapport between the necessity and the unavoidable reality of creolization, and the necessity and unavoidable reality of the *place*, that is to say, the place from which one speaks. One does not utter words in the air, casting them into empty air. The place from which one emits words, emits texts, makes one's voice heard, utters the cry – this place is immense. But one can close off this place, and one can enclose oneself within it. The site from which one utters the cry can be set up as a territory, that is, closed off by walls – spiritual, ideological, etc. walls. It then ceases to be a 'site'. The important thing today is precisely to be able to discuss a poetics of Relation in such a way as not to negate the place, not to dilute it, but to open it up. Do we have the means of doing this? Is it realizable by man, by the human race, by the human being? Or must we accept once and for all that in order to preserve the place we must preserve the exclusivity of place? I have not denied that there is a question there. But I have said that if we do not ask the question, we are perpetuating blind enclosures, and from blind enclosures we get the likes of Bosnia, Croatia, Serbia, and so on. No solution, whether political, economic, military or sociological, will resolve such problems until human beings' spirituality, mentality, intellectual powers swing in the opposite direction and start to ask this very question. Until then we will perpetuate impossible wars, pointless deaths and massacres everywhere. I have not denied that there is a problem, but I have said that one must address this problem.

Q. Can you tell us what you mean by 'Relation', by a poetics of 'Relation'?

É.G. In Western cultures, one says that the absolute is the absolute of being, and that being cannot be unless it is conceived as absolute. However, even as early as the pre-Socratics, it was accepted that being is relation, i.e. that being is not an absolute, that being is a relation to the other, a relation to the world, a relation to the cosmos. That was pre-Socratic thought, which is beginning to make a comeback. In a much less spiritual way, when some ecologists in the world today fight for their ideal, what do they say? They say: 'If you kill the rivers, if you kill the trees, if you kill the sky, if you kill the earth, then you kill mankind'. In other words, they establish a network of relations between human beings and their environment. What I am saying is that the notion of Being and of Being as an absolute is linked to the notion of identity as a 'single root', of identity as exclusive, and that if one imagines a 'rhizome-identity' – that is, a root, but which reaches out to meet other roots – then what becomes important is not so much each root's claim to be an absolute, but the mode, the manner in which it enters into contact with other roots: Relation. A poetics of Relation seems to me more obvious and more interesting today than a poetics of Being.

Q. How has Martinique experienced creolization?

É.G. Creolization has nothing to do with the politics of 'mixed blood': that would be a very literal and short-sighted point of view. We have experienced creolization in two contexts: the negative aspect of slavery and servitude, and nowadays another negative aspect which is assimilation into French culture. There is a very powerful thrust towards the assimilation of French culture in Martinique and Guadeloupe. But what I must say is that creolization, even when practiced in negative ways, nevertheless continues to advance. And 'inside' creolization, we have access to many ways of escaping the negativity. That is why, as you may have noticed, the Antilleans who live creolization are always drawn to other places: Marcus Garvey towards the blacks of the United States; Fanon towards Algeria; Césaire's texts on the whole of black Africa. George Padmore, Nkrumah's advisor in Africa, was a Trinidadian, etc. There is always a kind of expansion. As if, being perhaps unable to solve the problems at home, Caribbeans wanted to help other people, in an elsewhere that would still always be 'here'. That is the positive side: a painful way of living creolization, but a real way, which prefigures future solidarities.

Because they developed in a period when the model for identity was the single root, the Creole societies of the Caribbean, and more particularly of the francophone Antilles (where the processes of assimilation were at work with depressing visibility) tended to appear as a kind of lightness, a suspension of being, lacking in intensity. That was the view of two wanderers in search of an essence, a primordial truth, who landed on Martinique at the beginning of this century: Lafcadio Hearn and Paul Gauguin. The extreme joy and suffering of their quasi alchemical mutations, Hearn into a Japanese, Gauguin into an Oceanian – even if they realized that they were only roaming on the edges of an otherness that they desired to accommodate, to adopt – was in itself evidence that they could never have experienced or accepted the joy and the suffering of creolization, which perhaps seemed to them to engender affectation, dilapidation and loss of essence. That is why Hearn and Gauguin went off to search for weightier places, millennial traditions, a source, a permanence. This is also what the Rastas do, finding strength in the Ethiopian Rastafari mystique but without leaving the Caribbean. Just as in their time the most generous or most lucid of the Antilleans searched, Frantz Fanon for the absolute of Third World rebellion, Aimé Césaire the essentialist character of Negritude. The time had not yet come to engage with 'that which changes by exchanging'.

◆ 2 ◆

Languages and *langages**

I would like to make two general preliminary points about this meditation that I am embarking upon in your company. The first is that one can repeat things. I believe that repetition is one of the forms of knowledge in our world: it is through repeating things that one begins to glimpse the emergence of something new. The second concerns the commonplace. For me, commonplaces are not clichés, they are common places: literally places where the world's thoughts meet each other. We find ourselves writing, uttering or reflecting on an idea that we then come across, in an Italian or a Brazilian journal, in a different form, produced in a different context by someone whom we have nothing to do with. These are common places. That is, the places where one of the world's thoughts confirms another of the world's thoughts.

The highest subject that literature can give itself is what I call the 'chaos-world', and we are going to see how, for me, this truth is articulated. It is quite certain that even when it was exploiting or exploring the most secretly guarded recesses of the human being, and so neglecting that relation to the world that I am talking about, literature nevertheless was always, obviously, informed by a conception of the world. Under the surface of what appears to be the clearest of poems, we hear the muted music of a vision of the world. Poets have always claimed to be conscious of this relation to the 'world-totality' that alone can authorize its most innocent images. But it is only today, now that the world-totality is at last realized

---

* Lecture given at the Colloque sur les 'Sociétés et littératures antillaises, Université de Perpignan, 1994. English has no equivalent for the distinction between 'langue' and 'langage', which is an important element in Glissant's discussion of language use. He uses 'langage' to denote the speaker's subjective attitude to the 'langue' (French, English, Creole, etc.) that s/he uses.

concretely, geographically, that this vision of the world, which previously was 'prophetic' in literature, can fully come into play by taking as its actual subject matter that which previously was only its aim. When I say this, I am not claiming to propel literature into a kind of abstract generalization. To have a poetics of the world-totality means to link the place from which a literature is produced to the world-totality, and vice versa. In other words, literature does not come out of a vacuum, it is not just hanging in the air. It comes from a place, there is a crucial place from which the literary work is produced, but nowadays the work is all the more attached to the place in so far as it establishes a relation between that place and the world-totality.

A comparison will better allow me to approach this new dimension of literature. I think of the fate of the great books that marked the beginning of human communities. And at the beginning of all these communities, there is of course, irresistibly, the poetic cry. I want to talk about communities which were established one or several millennia ago, and which for convenience I will call *atavistic* communities (by which I mean the old communities of Asia, black Africa, Europe, and the Amerindian cultures). I think we talked about this last time, and we distinguished between these atavistic communities – that are based on the idea of a Genesis, i.e. a creation of the world, and the idea of a filiation, i.e. a continuous connection from the community's present back to this Genesis – and the composite cultures born of creolization, where any idea of Genesis can only be or have been imported, adopted or imposed: the true Genesis of the Caribbean peoples is the belly of the slave ship and the den of the Plantation.

And at the beginning of all these atavistic communities is the poetic cry: the Old Testament, the *Iliad* and the *Odyssey*, the *Song of Roland*, the *Nibelungen*, the Finnish *Kalevala*, the sacred books of India, the Icelandic Sagas, the *Popul Vuh* and the *Chilam Balam* of the Amerindians. Hegel, in Chapter 3 of his *Aesthetics*, characterizes this epic literature as a literature of the consciousness of the community, but a consciousness that is still naïve, in other words not yet political, at a moment when the community is not confident of its order, a moment when it needs to reassure itself with regard to its order (whether it be with the *Iliad*, the *Song of Roland* or the Old Testament). This poetic cry of the beginnings of consciousness is also the cry of an exclusive consciousness. That is, the traditional epic assembles everything that constitutes the community and excludes from it everything that is not the community. Of course this is even truer of other, more imperial (in every sense!) epic creations such as the *Aeneid* for the Roman Empire, the *Divine Comedy* for the Catholic universe, or more secretly poignant ones like Agrippa d'Aubigné's *Les Tragiques* for the Protestant consciousness, for example. These communities that are beginning to take shape formulate and project a poetic cry that gathers together the home, the place and the nature of the community and by the same token excludes from the community everything that is not the community. It is on the basis of these communitarian poetics that the specific forms of literature establish themselves: lyrical, philosophical, dramatic, fictional, etc. All these emerging varieties of the poetic cry gather together and mould the substance of a vulnerable community. For I believe – I may have said this last time – that the epic is the cry of a community that is not yet sure of its identity and traditionally needs this cry to reassure itself in the face of a threat. The epic has always been thought of as the glorifying of a victory, but I think it is the song that redeems a defeat or an ambiguous victory. It is quite clear that Roncevaux is a defeat for Charlemagne, and in the wake of that defeat the community rewrites the event in order to exorcize the defeat. When one considers the epic one always finds this need for reassurance. For example in the *Iliad*, the victory of the Greeks is not a triumph, it is based on a subterfuge. Had it not been for the wily Ulysses, they would still be outside the walls of Troy today. It's not a victory, it's a trick. And in the *Odyssey*, the epic is bitter. Ulysses coming home is recognized only by his dog. In the Icelandic Sagas, there is an extraordinary lamentation on the fate that weighs on the heroes.

I think that this kind of literature – probably the most accomplished that we have known, despite the developments of subsequent literatures – sums up what will subsequently happen in the literary domain. Because, on this basis, every literature will be considered by its community to have been dictated in the language (of the god) of the community. It is not the language of the god or gods of other communities and, in literary terms the language will acquire an absolute nature and a function of sacralization whose consequences will be perceptible right up to the present day. What precisely are we seeing happen today? The difficult birth of a different kind of community made up of the realized totality of all the communities of the world, realized in conflict, exclusion, massacres, intolerance, but realized nevertheless, because we are no longer dreaming of the world-totality, we are in sync with the world-totality, we are inside it. What for the traditional poet was a dream of unity or universalization becomes for us a difficult plunge into a chaos-world.

Once again, concerning the notion of chaos, when I say chaos-world, I will repeat what I have explained about creolization: the chaos-world exists because unpredictability exists. It is the idea of the unpredictability of the global relation that causes and creates the idea of the chaos-world. And our consciousness of this difficult birth of a new kind of community participation – in an impossible city that has been called 'village earth' (but every village still presupposes a hegemonic Centre) – is no longer naïve, as it was with the first founding texts of the world's communities, because politics has now become involved; and we cannot ignore this. We no longer have a naïve consciousness of it, but an anxious consciousness. Why this anxiety when faced with the reality of the chaos-world? Because we see quite clearly that the *non*-naïve consciousness of this totality can *no longer* be one that excludes, can no longer provide that sense of security bestowed, in the *Iliad* or the Old Testament, by the certainty of the chosen community establishing itself on a chosen ground that thus became its territory. For the non-naïve consciousness of this new total community asks itself: how can one be oneself without closing oneself to the other, and how can one accept the other, all the others, without renouncing oneself? That is the question that occupies the poet and that he has to address when he is in sync with *his* community, with the community that he has to support most of the time, because it is today a community that finds itself under threat in the world. But he must no longer defend his community by the dream of a world-totality that would be universally accepted (as in the past when this world-totality was still in the domain of dreams); he must defend his community in the reality of a chaos-world that no longer accepts generalizing universality.

There is this anxiety concerning the relation between self and other, and there is another question, another anxiety: in the abundant panorama of all the languages of the world today – and just as we are being drawn into another transition, no longer from the oral to the written but from the written to the oral – do we not see that we are no longer able to guarantee the formal uniqueness of our language, and that we all have to invent multiple forms whose baroque demands frighten us? The two questions are thus linked. Writing, the dictation of the gods, is linked to transcendence, it is linked to the immobility of the body and also to a sort of tradition of logical sequence that we can call a linear way of thinking. Orality and bodily movement go together with repetition, redundancy, the influence of rhythm, the renewal of associations, and all this takes us away from the transcendent thinking, and the sense of security that comes with transcendent thinking, and the sectarian excesses that it unleashes as a matter of course.

As we arrive at this point in our reflection or our meditation or our reverie, we cannot help seeing that this issue of transition from the written to the oral today is an important one, a crucial issue that raises the question of transcendence, raises the question of the absolute, and raises the question of Relation and relativism as opposed to the absolute. We observe that there are technical factors that lead to orality (everywhere we hear that books are becoming obsolete, etc.). But we also observe that oral cultures, oral civilizations that used to be crammed into the hidden face of the world are now appearing on 'the great stage of the world'. And as we examine the written and the oral today, we cannot avoid seeing that there are in fact two kinds of orality. There is the orality of the mass media, which is the orality of standardization and banalization. And then there is another form of orality that is vibrant and creative, which is that of those cultures that are now suddenly appearing on 'the great stage of the world' and which, also, do not choose the mode or the tool of written language as often as those of cinema, the visual and plastic arts, etc. but which are nonetheless oral cultures and manifestations of orality. I believe, for instance, that Haitian peasant painting, which is wrongly called naïve painting, is the painting of the Creole language, and that there is a link between Haitian Creole orality and Haitian peasant painting. And this question of writing and orality produces a stimulating anxiety in the poet, the writer. He has to find answers to two interconnected problems: firstly, how his community can express itself in relation to the world-totality, and, secondly, how his community can express itself in a quest for both the absolute and the non-absolute, or for writing and orality. The poet must create a synthesis of all that: and it is this, in my view, that is exciting and complex in the current panorama of the languages and literatures of the world. This creative anxiety is the opposite of the pessimism or 'metaphysical' despair born of the thinking of 'Being'.

I speak and above all I write in the presence of all the world's languages. Many languages are dying out in the world today – for example in black Africa, languages are disappearing because their speakers are being absorbed into a larger national community; or because the language is no longer a language of peasant production, or of any kind of production, and so is being eroded; or simply because the language's users are physically disappearing from the country in which they lived – but we know that we write in the presence of all the world's languages, even if we do not know any of them. To use myself as an example, I am imbued, poetically imbued, with this necessity even though I have terrible difficulty in speaking any other language than those that I use (Creole and French). But writing in the presence of all the world's languages does not mean knowing all the world's languages. It means that in the current context of literatures and of the relation between poetics and the chaos-world, I can no longer write in a monolingual way. Rather, I take my own language and I shake it up and shift it around, not into syntheses, but into linguistic openings that enable me to conceive of the relations between languages today on the surface of the planet – relations of dominance, of complicity, absorption, oppression, erosion, contact, etc. – as a huge *drama*, a huge tragedy from which my own language cannot remain exempt and safe. And as a result I cannot write my language in a monolingual manner; I write it in the presence of this tragedy, this drama. We will not save one of the world's languages by letting the others die. This means that in the present dramatic relationship between languages, just as I can no longer write monolingually, so I can no longer defend my language monolingually. I must defend it in the awareness that it is not the only language under threat in the world (even if it is Creole that concerns me the most – if you like, we can leave for the discussion the question that I am sure you will ask me: why don't you write in Creole if it is your mother tongue?).

A new perspective is opening up for an Antillean like me, who belongs to a country in which there is a dominant language, French, and a dominated language, Creole: it is that in the global tragedy of languages, here French and Creole ultimately support each other. Although one does dominate the other, we have had to make the effort to understand that this domination, although real, is a second or even third degree domination in the global tragedy of languages. We have come to a moment in history where we see that human imagination needs all the world's languages and that, as a kind of consequence, in the crucial place from where the literary work is produced, in the Antilles, the Antillean human imagination needs Creole *and* French. Moreover this is why I have never been able to agree with the sort of vague rallying that is the francophone movement. This crucial dimension has to be included in the practice and learning of every language. I repeat that multilingualism does not presuppose the coexistence of languages, nor the knowledge of several languages, but the presence of the world's languages in the practice of one's own; that is what I call multilingualism.

This means that we have to distinguish between the language that we use and the *langage*, that is to say the relationship to words, that we construct in literature and poetry. I will sum this up by saying that the defence of the language is absolutely necessary because it is this that allows us to oppose standardization, the standardization that would result for example from a universalization of basic Anglo-American. I say that if this standardization ever became a reality, it is not only French or Italian or Creole that would be under threat, but above all the English language, because English would cease to be a language with its obscurities, its weaknesses, its triumphs, its bursts of energy, its retreats and its diversity; it would cease to be the language of the peasant, the language of the writer, of the seaman, etc. All of that would disappear, English would cease to be a living language and would become a kind of international code, an Esperanto. If English was my language, I would be worried about the universalization and standardization of Anglo-American.

Defending the language is crucial, and it is by this defence that one opposes standardization. And it is also by this defence that one opposes dilution, since, to repeat what was emphasized last time, the poetics of Relation is not a poetics of the jumbled up, the undifferentiated, the neutral. For there to be a relation there must be two or more identities or entities that are sovereign, and that agree to change by exchanging. Second consideration: the defence of the language, let me repeat, entails the defence of all the world's languages. But the construction of a *langage* in the language one uses opens it up towards the chaos-world: because this sets up relations between the possible languages of the world. Let me take the case of the Antilles, where a *langage* is the manifestation of our relation to the language, of our attitude towards the world, an attitude of confidence or reserve, of profusion or silence, of openness to the world or of closing oneself off from the world, of developing the techniques of orality or of closing ranks around the ancient demands of writing, or else a symbiosis of all this. A *langage* has thus appeared in the Caribbean, weaving its way across the English, French, Spanish and Creole languages of the Caribbean universe and perhaps also of South America. In a conversation we had not long before his death, Alejo Carpentier said to me 'We Caribbeans write in four or five different languages but we have the same *langage*'. The art of the Creole storyteller is made up of driftings and also accumulations, with that baroque quality in the sentences, those distortions of discourse where what is inserted acts as a natural breathing space, that circularity of the narrative and that tireless repetition of the theme. All of that comes together into a *langage* that runs across the languages of the Caribbean, English, Creole, Spanish or French – the language of Carpentier, of Walcott, or the francophone writers of Martinique, Guadeloupe or Haiti. And the wonderful thing is, you see, that this exploration of a *langage* through and beyond the various languages used in no way perverts any of them, but, convening them all in one focal point, adds to each a place of mystery and magic where, meeting together, they finally 'understand' each other.

In the past, in the time of those founding texts that I have talked about and all the literatures that proceeded from them, thought – what I call systematic thought – organized, studied and projected these slow, imperceptible repercussions between languages, and predicted and put into an ideological perspective the movement of the world that they legitimately governed. Today, this systematic thought, which I also like to call 'continental thought', has failed to account for the generalized non-system of the world's cultures. Another form of thought is developing, more intuitive, more fragile, threatened, but in tune with the chaos-world and its unpredictability, perhaps supported by discoveries in the human and social sciences but stemming from a vision of the poetics and the imagination of the world. I call this thought 'archipelagic', that is non-systematic, inductive thought that explores the unexpected in the world-totality and reconciles writing with orality and orality with writing. What I see today is that the continents are turning themselves into archipelagos, at least from the point of view of an outsider. The Americas are 'archipelagizing', they are forming themselves into regions across national frontiers. And I think that this is a term whose dignity should be restored: the term *region*. Europe is 'archipelagizing'. The linguistic and cultural regions, crossing the barriers between nations, are islands, but open islands, and that is the principal condition for their survival. Systematic thought, continental thought, the old ideological thought that forecast the world, valued the vernacular languages – that we will now call regional languages, if we give a new, exhaustive meaning to the term region – in so far as they were languages of imprisonment, of turning in on oneself, of folklore and of inert particularism. This immediately creates certain tasks for us, and the conclusion is clear: all these languages must agree with each other [s'entendre] across space, in the three senses of 's'entendre': they must listen to each other, understand each other, and get on well with each other. Listening to the other, to the others, means enlarging the spiritual dimension of one's own language, that is to say, putting it in relation. Understanding the other, the others, means accepting that the truth from elsewhere complements the truth from here. And getting on well with the other means agreeing to add to the particular strategies developed to benefit each regional or national language, more general strategies that would be worked out in common. It seems to me that in the panorama of the world today it is the mission of the poet, the writer and the intellectual to reflect and to come up with proposals with regard to all these coordinates, all these relations, all these intertwinings of the question of languages.

To finish I would like to make a few brief comments on what I consider to be one of the most important arts of the future: the art of translation. What all translations now imply in their very principle, in the very passage that they enact from one language to another, is the sovereignty of all the world's languages. And translation, for that very reason, is the sign and the proof that we have to conceive of this totality of languages in our imagination. Just as the writer now realizes this totality in the practice of *his* language of expression, so the translator manifests it in the passage from *one* language to another, in the face of the uniqueness of each of these languages. But, just as in our chaos-world one will not save any of the world's languages by letting the others perish, the translator can establish a relation between two languages – two systems of uniqueness – only in the presence of all the others, their powerful presence in his imagination, even if he does not know any of them. What does this mean if not that, just as the poet invents a *langage* in his own language, the translator has to invent a *langage* going between one language and the other? A necessary *langage* going from one language to the other, a *langage* common to both of them, but in some sense unforeseeable with regard to each of them. The translator's *langage* works like creolization and Relation in the world, that is, it produces the unforeseeable. An art of the imaginary, in this sense translation is a true operation of creolization, from now on a new and unstoppable practice of our precious cultural hybridity. An art of the crossing of hybridities aspiring to the world-totality, a vertiginous art of salutary wanderings, translation is progressively writing itself into the multiplicity of our world. Translation is therefore one of the most important kinds of this new archipelagic thinking. It is an art of the flight ['fugue'] from one language to another, in which neither the first nor the second are effaced. But also an art of fugue in that every translation now forms part of the network of all possible translations from and into all languages.

If it is true that with every language that dies a part of the human imagination also dies, it is also true that with every language which is translated that imagination is enriched in a manner both fixed and wandering. Translation is a flight, in other words a beautiful relinquishing. This is what one must perhaps above all discern in the act of translation. It is true that the poem, when translated into another language, loses some of its rhythm, its assonances, the chance that is both the accident and the permanence of writing. But one must perhaps accept this, accept this relinquishing. Because in fact, in the world-totality, it equates with the part of oneself that in every poetics one gives up to the other. I will say that this relinquishing, when it is supported by sufficient reasons and inventions, when it leads into this *langage* of sharing that I have spoken about, is the thinking of the light touch, the archipelagic thinking whereby we recompose the world's landscapes, a thought which, against all the kinds of systematic thought, teaches us the uncertain, the threatened, but also the poetic intuition in which we can now move ahead. Translation, the art of the light touch and the approach, is a practice of the trace. Against the absolutist limitation of Being, the art of translation works to accumulate the expanse of all the beings and all the existences in the world. Creating traces in languages means creating traces in the unforeseeable of what is now our common condition.

QUESTIONS

Pierre Nepveu. I would like to ask you about this presence of other languages. You say: 'I write in the presence of all the world's languages, even if I do not know them'. How do you define this presence, what kind of presence is it, how does it manifest itself, in what modalities?

É.G. It obviously does not manifest itself in linguistic terms. What I mean is that in the traditions of the literatures of the world, and whether they are oral or written, the function of the poet has always been, more or less visibly, to affirm the exclusive uniqueness of the community, or of what can be considered the community, in relation to all other possible communities, on the one hand. On the other hand, it is perfectly clear that almost all the world's literatures have been supported by the idea that the language of the community is a chosen language. In the West, and particularly in Europe, the literary function is viewed, unconsciously, as a function deriving from the dictation of a god. You can call this inspiration, you can call it whatever you like, but the implication is always that the word, the language, has been dictated by a god, the god of the community, that the language is transcendent and that the writing of this language is a form of transcendence. It is in the name of this transcendence that all oral literatures have been despised, dominated, rejected, oppressed and pushed into the shadows, and that people have thought that all oral cultures are inferior to the cultures of writing. Writing is the sign of uniqueness and of the divine. In this context the writer, up until the nineteenth century, writes monolingually. Bear in mind that Voltaire thought that Shakespeare was a 'savage', and that people as intelligent as the English writers of that period said that Racine was a wimp, because it was impossible to conceive of Shakespeare in the poetics of the French language and equally impossible for an English person to conceive of Racine; writers stuck to their monolingual path. Nowadays the problems have shifted. There is a problem regarding the roots of communities, because in most parts of the world they have been dominated by the act of colonization, but there is also a problem of Relation. We can see this in all domains: political, economic, etc. When a butterfly flaps its wings in the Tokyo stock exchange there are 'ecological' catastrophes in the stock exchanges in London and Paris. We see that there are relations, but we don't see Relation, as far as the cultural expression of communities is concerned. Nevertheless Relation is present, it exists. Whether I like it or not, whether I accept it or not – some people do and others don't – I am determined by a certain number of relations in the world. Every time I have been to California I have been afraid of earthquakes. But there are earthquakes in my own country and when I am there I am not afraid. But when I am in California I am afraid of earthquakes, because I have seen earthquakes in California on television whereas I have never seen earthquakes in *my* country on television. And I am not afraid of earthquakes in my country. When I am in Martinique, I *never* think about earthquakes. And when the earthquake arrives, I do not panic, I try to get into the open, not to stand under a beam; I know more or less what to do. Just as we know how to defend ourselves, all night if necessary, against a hurricane, and we know what to do. But when I am in California, in a hotel, and I can feel the rumbling of the quake, I do panic, because there is this problem of the relation in the sensibility, in the culture. It is no longer the political, economic or military relation, but there is this thing that happens, that affects me whether I like it or not. And it is certain that if I write a text in California, it will be different from a text that I would write in Martinique. It will be suspended in the quake. It will have a different connotation; I no longer write monolingually. I write with this nexus of relations, and I repeat that it is not a question of knowing or using other languages. The language that I most enjoy speaking is Italian, because when I speak Italian I am not worried about making mistakes. I don't at all mind making mistakes in Italian; there is a pleasure in speaking Italian, and making or not making mistakes doesn't matter at all to me. But when I speak English I'm always thinking: oh no! perhaps I have made a mistake there; and suddenly I am stuck. That is the problem of Relation (perhaps together with the weight of my prejudices), which has nothing to do with the fact of speaking or not speaking, knowing or not knowing, being obliged or not obliged to speak a language, but which is the current situation of the world, the current situation of cultural relations and relations of sensibility, of aesthetics (and of languages) in the world today. And that is why I say that I write in the presence of all the world's languages. In Strasbourg once, during one of the sessions of the International Writers' Parliament, there was a very beautiful poetry reading, where I read a French translation of some poems by Beidao, who is a Chinese poet, and he read them in Chinese, and Adonis* had translated one of my texts into Arabic, which he read, and I read my texts from *Indes* or *Sel noir*, I can't remember which, in French. And Adonis read his texts in Arabic, and someone else read the French translations of them. There was also a poet who writes in French, André Velter, and a poet who writes in Hebrew, Nathan Zach, who exchanged their texts and their translations with the others. It was in a church and it was incredible. There was a sort of silence and aura and everyone was very aware of everyone else. Of course, we had to use translation to achieve this. But we heard the words, and we understood without understanding. Something new was growing on the stage of the world, something that we must take into account when we think about poetics now.

Q. You have spoken about creolization and you have also spoken about the baroque. I don't know if these two concepts are co-extensive for you, or if you distinguish between them? I myself think that creolization has its own specificity, a specificity that stems firstly from the nature of the cultures that it brings together, secondly from the physical context, and thirdly from the power that has brought about this hybridity. I mean that for Antillean poetics, for instance, there is the fact of the violence of the colonization that results in the specificity of this poetics. There is violence everywhere, whatever form this encounter takes, but I think the violence that has produced this hybridity in the Antilles gives a particular character to Antillean poetics. I don't know if I am wrong?

É.G. Both assertions are true. The connection between them is perhaps not true. Creolization is always a manifestation of the baroque because the baroque is that which is opposed, let's say, to classicism. What is classicism? For any literature, any culture? It is the moment when that literature or that culture proposes its particular values as universal values. The baroque is the anti-classical, that is, baroque thought says that there are no universal values, that every value is a particular value to be put in

---

* Adonis is the pen name of the Syrian poet Ali Ahmad Said Esber.

relation with another particular value and that as a result it is impossible for any particular value to legitimately consider itself or present itself and impose itself as a universal value. It can impose itself as a universal value through force, but not legitimately. That is what baroque thought states, and in this sense all creolization is a form of the baroque, you see, in action. Moreover the baroque, which was initially a reaction to the Counter-Reformation in Europe, has become naturalized all over the world. When the baroque crossed the oceans and arrived in Latin America, the angels and virgins became black, Jesus Christ was an Indian, and all that broke up the processes of legitimacy. The baroque was naturalized. Creolization is always baroque. Nowadays, creolization may or may not happen in violent forms. I don't know if violence is necessarily associated with creolization. I don't think so. Creolization includes violence, and in the fullest sense of the word 'include', that is to say it integrates violence. The fact that there has been violence in the plantation system does not mean that there has been no creolization – on the contrary. And on that I am in agreement with you. Does that imply a necessary association? It is true that it determines a characteristic, but I don't think that this characteristic amounts to a necessary association. In other words there can be creolizations without violence, it seems to me that there can be creolizations without violence. However, I am trying to think of examples and I can't find any!

Q. I would like you to go back to the choice you have made of the French language rather than the Creole language. And I would like to know if your works have been translated into Creole?

É.G. Some poems, yes, have been translated by Creole poets. I will reply to you by means of an anecdote. After the anecdote, I will perhaps make a few comments. The anecdote is that poets writing in Creole today, for example in Guadeloupe, have sometimes said to me: if you, along with others, had not shaken up, disturbed, broken down the French language in your works, perhaps we would not have dared to write in Creole because we would have still been stunned at the idea of 'disrespecting', as we say at home, this French language. In other words, this: that the 'creolization' of the French language goes hand in hand with the liberation of the Creole language.

Now, I think that we are truly, in Martinique and Guadeloupe – perhaps less so today in Haiti – a bilingual society, that is to say, there is a real presence of the Creole language which is spoken by 100% of the population, and a real presence of the French language which is spoken by

95% of the population. For this reason Creole is also in contact with French (we saw this last time: it is a vocabulary of eighteenth-century Breton and Norman seamen 'matched' to a syntax that has nothing to do with this; probably a synthesis of the syntaxes of the west coast of black Africa), and this contact between Creole and French constitutes the originality of the French-speaking Antillean cultures. We must make Creole opaque in relation to French or de-structure French in relation to Creole in order to master both of them, in order to get away from 'pidgin French'. We must establish the originality of Creole in relation to French, and the originality of French in relation to Creole (creolization is in no way a mish-mash). This is what I have tried to do in my literary work. Now, it is a question of generations: perhaps if today I were twenty years old I would start by writing in Creole. But one part of the work on literature that I have achieved has been to practise this poetics of 'non-contact' between Creole and French.

Q. When you were talking about the relationship between the written and the oral, and following on from what you have said just now, do the works of Confiant and Chamoiseau belong in that general area? Like *Texaco*, etc.

É.G. Probably, but I am not sure. It would take a long time to discuss this fully. I read Saint-John Perse's *Éloges* and I see how the text is to some extent creolizing but that the creolization in it is hidden. The poet does it but hides it. For example, about a scene of the sea he says: 'Ces cayes, nos maisons', etc. A 'caye' is a collection of rocks breaching the surface of the sea, or the foam of waves breaking against these rocks. Fishermen go there because there are fish among the rocks about a kilometre out from the beaches ... 'Ces cayes, nos maisons ...' No-one notices. But 'caye' in Martinican Creole is 'case', in other words, 'house'. And no-one realizes that he is saying: 'Ces *cayes*, nos *maisons* ...' and the text goes on. That is to say, he comes up with a creolization, and then camouflages it! It's an apposition, take it or leave it, see it or don't. And there are dozens of examples like this in Saint-John Perse. There are some obvious creolizations: when he says: 'pour moi, j'ai retiré mes pieds' ['as for me, I left'], which is the literal translation of the Creole expression: 'man tiré pyé moin'. That is obvious. But there are other creolizations, when for example he says: 'Ces filles, là ...' ['those girls, there'] and then goes on. 'Tifitala' in Creole, and the French 'là' is there as a creolization of the text, but camouflaged. Whereas with Chamoiseau and Confiant the creolization is openly proclaimed. In other words, it is a different operation; it is proclaimed and is part of a whole overt system and a manifest intention. I think I perhaps prefer the poetics of Saint-John Perse, his camouflage of creolization, to this practice of loudly proclaiming the creolization of the 'text'. But creolization is infinitely open-ended, and these writers you refer to are fruitfully unpredictable, and we have not yet begun to really appreciate the merits of their ways of working.

P.N. You say that everything is 'Relation', and that there is a difficult linguistic imbalance at work, Creole–French, French–English, etc. and you have cited Shakespeare. I wonder if in your description of this artistic creation on the level of languages one could not cite more popular authors? The creators of rap for instance. Do we not find there a phenomenon that is very close to creolization through the creation of a survival strategy, a linguistic anthropophagy? One has killed the language but … I love you, I eat you and I understand you.

É.G. Yes, except that in the *langage* of rap as in the *langage* of Jamaican dub poetry, Michael Smith or Linton Kwesi Johnson, as in certain other forms of *langage* that appear in linguistic and cultural microclimates like Miami for example, it is a case of the deliberate and aggressive deformation of a language from within this language. Michael Smith or Linton Kwesi Johnson or Edward Kamau Brathwaite (the Jamaican poet)* write – Michael Smith has sent me some wonderful poems – in this language which is … what can we call it? I used to say a pidgin, but I quickly stopped using that term, because when I proposed it once at a conference in Jamaica, my Jamaican friends protested strongly. And they told me, no, that's not possible, you cannot call that language a pidgin. And that's right, we can't call it a pidgin, but the fact remains that it is an aggressive deformation – cultural, militant, deliberate – within *one* language, and a challenging of the normative uniqueness of that language, carried out by a group of people whom one knows, and one knows when they started this practice, and one perhaps knows when they will stop doing it. Whereas creolization, I repeat, occurs when two or more heterogeneous linguistic spheres are brought into contact with a result that is unforeseeable. No-one knows who creates the creolization, not of the 'text' but of the language in general, we don't know when the Creole language was born, nor by whom, nor how. We know when rap or dub poetry were born, and by whom and how. In other

---

* Brathwaite is in fact Barbadian.

words, regarding the ravages (in a good sense) that are produced in rap or dub poetry or other similar kinds of expression, I wonder if one could not for example link them to Joual, as this was spoken aggressively, culturally, politically, in Quebec. In each case, rap or dub poetry or Joual, the same phenomenon of challenging uniqueness is at work. And as a result, such practices ultimately meet up with the duplications (the positive duplicities) of the Creole languages.

Gaston Miron. It is not only the poet who can save a language. Concretely, what can we do? I was reading in *Le Devoir* recently that almost twelve thousand languages are spoken in the world, but that in thirty to fifty years' time there will be only six thousand; half of these languages are going to disappear, this is certain. What can we do? This is a frightening impoverishment of the imagination!

É.G. I think there are two orders of questions. There is the question of what one could call the everyday struggles, that is, when one is in a given place, one has to adapt one's daily life to the conditions of that place. And if daily life involves fighting for this or that, if the daily life of a Quebecker involves fighting for the preservation of the Quebec language, and if the daily life of a Martiniquan involves fighting for the preservation of a Creole, then that can mean working with all sorts of cultural, political or militant organizations. But I also think that these political or cultural battles that we have all fought and continue to fight take place within a global context such that one must, at the same time as fighting this kind of battle, also change the direction of poetics, contribute to changing the mentality of human beings, abandon the 'if you are not like me you are my enemy, if you are not like me I am allowed to fight you': it seems to me that this is one of the functions of the poet – and not only the poet, the artist – to contribute to the overthrow of this order of things. No longer to just leave it to humanism, kindness, tolerance, which are so fleeting, but to enter into the decisive mutations of a plurality to which we all consent. This will take a long time but in the global relation of our times one of the most obvious tasks of literature, poetry and art is to contribute to the gradual 'unconscious' acceptance by human beings that the other is not the enemy, that what is different does not undermine me, that if I change as a result of contact with it that does not mean that I am diluting myself in the other, etc. It seems to me that this is a different form of struggle from the daily battles, and that the artist is one of the best placed to carry it out; I believe this. Because the artist is someone who approaches the world's imagination, and the ideologies of the world, the visions of the world, the predictions, the ambitious plans are beginning to fail, and this new imagination must begin to rise up. This is no longer to dream of the world, it is to enter it.

✦ 3 ✦

Culture and Identity*

We need to go back over what I put forward in my first lecture. In particular, what we know about the problems of identity. When I introduced this question, I started from the distinction made by Deleuze and Guattari between the single root and the notion of the rhizome. In one of the chapters of *Mille Plateaux* (which was first published as a small volume under the title *Rhizomes*) Deleuze and Guattari emphasize this difference. They establish it from the point of view of the functioning of thought, the thought of the root and the thought of the rhizome. The single root is that which kills everything around it whereas the rhizome is the root that reaches out to meet other roots. I applied this image to the principle of identity. And I did so also with regard to a 'categorization of cultures', which is my own idea, to a division of cultures into the *atavistic* and the *composite*. I think we have already spoken about this last time and the time before that. The notion of identity as single root – which has not always been a deadly notion, which has produced some magnificent works in the history of humanity – is linked to the very nature of what I call atavistic cultures. And I have already explained that for me the atavistic culture is that which starts from the principle of a Genesis and the principle of a filiation, with the aim of seeking legitimacy on a land which, from that moment onwards, becomes a territory. I will make this equation: 'chosen land = territory'. We all know the ethnic devastation caused by this magnificent and deadly conception. I have linked the principle of rhizomatic identity to the existence of composite cultures, that is, cultures in which creolization is practiced. But in these cultures, very often, we find ourselves confronted with an opposition between the atavistic and the composite. I analysed

---

* Lecture given at the Journées antillaises des universités de Bologne et de Parme, 1994. (In these texts, Glissant sometimes speaks as though they were a continuous series, all to the same audience, and one may guess that he made a number of other alterations to the original lectures.)

this, for example, in connection with the ways in which the Americas were composed and populated. If we consider a country like Mexico, we immediately see that there is there an atavistic culture, i.e. that of the Amerindians of Mexico – the culture of the Chiapas – and a composite culture, which is the general culture of the Mexican nation today. And we see that there is an opposition between the two.

One can ask oneself whether there has not been an opposition between atavistic Amerindian cultures, in Canada and Quebec, and a social formation that without being creolized or composite is nevertheless different from these atavistic cultures. And each time, the question arises of the opposition, in these new countries or these countries of creolization, between the remains, the persistence of atavistic culture and this new process of creolization. In general, this is not a problem in the Caribbean, because the Amerindians there have all been exterminated, with the exception of a very small number who live in a reservation on the island of Dominica. The atavistic remnant of the Caribbean persists as a sort of unconscious trace. It would seem that for us Creoles of the Caribbean there is a sort of unconscious trace of this Amerindian existence. But in any case there is no ethnic conflict because the actual reality of Amerindian atavism has disappeared. In one of my books, *Le Discours antillais*, I analysed the case of a young man suffering from mental illness and treated in Paris, with no real understanding: one of his obsessions was that he was descended from a Carib chief, a great Carib chief. And I remember that forty or fifty years ago, Antilleans living in France would often claim that they were descended from the Caribs in order to escape from the African part of themselves, of which they were probably ashamed, under the cultural pressure of the colonizer. In any case, we can now see that in the countries of atavistic culture, ethnic opposition usually leads to massacre and genocide. And we can see that in the Americas the Amerindian atavistic cultures have generally been destabilized by the constitution of new countries, that is, their creolization. I don't know if this is the case in Quebec and Canada, but it is the case in Mexico, it is the case in Peru and in Columbia. The Caribbean also offers the example of populations from atavistic cultures that *have been deported there*: the Hindus, employed since 1830 as indentured workers. They have resisted culturally, but have also adapted to their new country. Creole *and* Hindu. The problem we are faced with is knowing how to change the imagination, the mentality and the intellect of human beings today, in such a way that within the atavistic cultures ethnic conflicts no longer appear as absolutes, and that within the creolized countries, ethnic and nationalistic conflicts no longer appear as unstoppable necessities.

Among the myths that have led towards the consciousness of History with a capital H, and here I return to the very principle of atavistic cultures (a Genesis and a filiation), we must distinguish between those that one could call founding myths and the others, which are myths of elucidation, of subterranean explanations, of connecting together and perhaps putting *en abyme** the various elements of the social structure in a given culture. The main role of the founding myths is to consecrate the presence of a community in a territory, by attaching, through legitimate filiation, this presence, this present time, to a Genesis, to a creation of the world. The founding myth provides an obscure kind of reassurance as to the unbroken continuity of this filiation and so authorizes the community in question to consider this land that has become a territory as absolutely its own. Through an extension of legitimacy – as we have also said – it can happen that, moving from myth to historical consciousness, the community then considers that it has the right to expand the limits of this territory. This is one of the bases of colonial expansion, which was closely linked to the idea of universality, in other words above all to the generalized legitimization of an absolute that was at the outset based on a particular chosen one, in a particular chosen one. One can understand why it is important that the founding myth anchors itself in a Genesis and consists of two driving forces: filiation and legitimacy, which guarantee its power and presuppose its aim: the universal legitimization of the community's presence. Isn't this the model according to which what we call History functions, whatever the philosophy that otherwise underpins it?

History is therefore in a real sense the daughter of the founding myth. Along the way that leads to it the founding myth will be accompanied, then masked, then replaced first by myths of elucidation, explanation or *mise en abyme* of a community's social processes and the conditions of its environment, then by the folk tales and narratives that prefigure its History, and finally by the novels, poems and essays that speak, sing or reflect on this. So that wherever founding myths appear, within these cultures that I have called atavistic, the notion of identity will develop around the axis of filiation and legitimacy: in depth, it is the single root that excludes the other as participant. One can infer from this that these cultures will maintain a conception (for instance of orality as prefiguration of the ontological approach) that will reach its natural conclusion in that accomplishment of the absolute that writing, writings, will become.

---

* 'Mise en abyme' is a term used in literary criticism to refer to a particular image in a text that mirrors the text as a whole.

What would historical consciousness be if not the generalized feeling of a mission to accomplish, a filiation to maintain, a legitimacy to preserve, or a territory to enlarge? As for those societies in which no founding myth functions, except through borrowing – by which I mean composite societies, societies of creolization – the notion of identity is realized around the weavings of Relation, which includes the other as an inference. These cultures start directly with the folk tale, which, paradoxically, is also a practice of detour, of turning away. What the folk tale thus turns away is the propensity to attach oneself to a Genesis, is the inflexibility of filiation, is the shadow cast by foundational legitimacies. And when the orality of the folk tale is carried over into the fixity of writing, as with the writers of the Caribbean and Latin America, it retains this luminous detour which will determine a different configuration of the written that will have expelled the ontological absolute. What then will historical consciousness be, if not the chaotic drive towards these conjunctions of all histories, none of which – and this is one of the major qualities of chaos – can any longer claim an absolute legitimacy? Atavistic cultures and composite cultures face the same situation, there is no point in referring to the former or praising the latter if one does not intend to go beyond them. Today, we have to reconcile the writing of myth and the writing of the folk tale, the memory of Genesis and the prescience of Relation, and that is a difficult task. But what other task would be nobler?

I would like to give you a concrete example. That of the Roma, or Romany of Europe, in other words, that of the Gypsies. The Roma, let's say the Gypsies for the sake of simplicity, are organizing a conference for peace in Sarajevo, in two or three months. I am bringing this up here because in the texts I have received there is a sort of principled stance that seemed to me an extremely good illustration of the point of view that I have just outlined to you so briefly. And I would like to read you a few extracts from this declaration of the Gypsies of Europe, a few quite brief but significant extracts. They write to the mayor of Sarajevo: 'On this the thousandth day of the siege, we reaffirm to you all our solidarity and our hope. It is because we believe in a free and multi-ethnic Sarajevo that we ask you to welcome the Congress for Peace that the International Romany Union is planning. Before the war, the Roma of Sarajevo enjoyed rights that they did not have elsewhere, such as the right to their language, and access to radio and television.' In another passage, they define themselves, they define the Roma, like this: 'all those who struggle for a multi-ethnic democracy'. In another passage, they say: 'The Roma are invisible in this war as in all wars, yet there were a million of them in ex-Yugoslavia. What has happened to the Yugoslavian Roma? What international aid are they receiving under the bombardment of Sarajevo and elsewhere? How are they getting enough food in a period of general famine and galloping inflation in the countries at war? Who has thought of a humanitarian convoy for the Roma of Bosnia? What cultural corridor has been opened for them, to let them breathe for a few days in the West in between two bursts of shelling? And what will become of them in the council for peace-making in ex-Yugoslavia? Will they still be deprived of their citizenship, as 25% of the Macedonian Roma are today? What kind of welcome will they receive where they take refuge? Will their houses continue to be razed to the ground in their absence by municipal bulldozers as happened on 15 July 1994 in the town of Zrenjanin in Vojvodina? Let us remind you that houses belonging to Roma living in the village of Baku twenty-three kilometres from Bucharest were set on fire and destroyed on the night of 7–8 January 1995, the day of an Orthodox religious festival, and following a confrontation between these Romanian villagers and Roma who had settled in the village. The Baku conflict is one of a series of about thirty similar incidents in Romania since January 1990. In several incidents of this type, the over-excited crowd rushed towards the houses of the Roma families to the sound of a tocsin. These scenarios are nothing other than contemporary versions of the pogroms that used to be traditional in Central and Western Europe. They illustrate the general predicament of the Roma, who have always been subjected to all the various kinds of discrimination and, in the present case, accused of all kinds of "ethnic impurities". The Roma Union is calling for this congress not in order to reproduce a historical division between the Roma and others, but on the contrary because only peace will confer on everyone a multicultural citizenship based on the diversity of cultures and the equality of rights. This peace congress will lay the foundations of tomorrow's multicultural citizenship, reflecting Roma culture which is tolerant, mixed-race, open to the world and at the same time singular. A utopia to which the Roma invite you all.' I emphasize 'mixed-race', 'open to the world' and 'at the same time singular'. And I will read just one last passage from this appeal: 'In order that the congress be not just a congress of Roma, or a congress of Yugoslavs, we must articulate the multi-ethnicity and the future of a possible policy which the Roma invite you to support. A non-territorial coexistence that goes beyond the obsolete spaces of a Europe in transformation, the Congress is a determinedly political congress in that it affirms civilization against barbarity, a civilization of which the Roma remind the world: movement, art, life, tolerance, hospitality, welcome, hybridity, creolization, which do not prevent singularity and identity. The Roma are a singular culture in the world, unlike any other, and yet they share with their hosts a large number of their cultural features: religion, language, customs, local destinies.'

I have read you these extracts because, in the course of my first lecture, the question arose of the relevance of the term 'creolization' in the context of the world-totality. And now I find this same term in the text of a solemn appeal made by the Roma of Central Europe – an appeal which they send out to the world – and I find not only the idea of hybridity, and in fact the idea of the rhizome-identity, but also the idea of openness to the world, and finally the idea that all this does not contradict singularity or identity. I am pleased on the one hand to bring this appeal by the Roma to your attention, and on the other hand to show that it is a concrete example of the necessity, of course, of supporting political and social struggles in the places in which one finds oneself, but also that of opening up everyone's imagination to something else, which is that we will not change anything in the situation of the peoples of the world unless we change that imagination, unless we change the idea that identity must be a single root, fixed and intolerant.

To live the world-totality from the place that is one's own means to establish a relation, not to sanction exclusion. I believe that literature, around this question of identity, is entering a period in which it will produce epics, new contemporary epics. All atavistic cultures, as we have said, have started with epic literature. We have cited the great foundational books of humanity. From the Old Testament to the *Iliad*, from the Egyptian *Book of the Dead* to the Indian *Bhagavad-Gîtâ*, from the Icelandic Sagas to the *Chanson de Roland*, from the *Aeneid* to the *Popul Vuh* or the *Chilam Balam* of the Amerindians, to the *Kalevala* of the Finns, the great epic books on which humanity is founded are books that reassure the community as to its own destiny and which as a result tend, not in themselves but in the use that is made of them, to exclude those that do not belong to this community. I say 'not in themselves', because these great books that have founded communities, that provide communities with their roots, are in fact books of wandering ['errance']. And if one examines the Old Testament, the *Iliad*, the sagas, the *Aeneid*, one sees straight away that these books are 'complete' because even within their calling for rootedness, they are also, directly, a call to wandering. And it seems to me that a new, contemporary, epic literature will start to appear as soon as the totality-world begins to be perceived as a new kind of community. However, we cannot fail to realize that this contemporary epic literature will, contrary to the great founding books of atavistic humanity, be expressed in a multilingual *langage* within the language that will enable its realization. This epic literature will also exclude the need for an expiatory victim such as one sees in the founding books of atavistic humanity. The victim and the expiation are the means of excluding everything that is not redeemed by them. Or else of 'universalizing', wrongly. The new epic literature will establish relation and not exclusion.

In the end, this epic literature will perhaps be able to do without the notion of Being, and to marvel instead at the imagination of the being, of all the possible beings in the world, of all the possible existents in the world. The question of Being will no longer be posed in that profitable solitude to which the thought of the universal has been reduced. The universal has toppled [*basculé*] into diversity, which shakes it up [*le bouscule*]. And this means that the question of Being can no longer base its legitimacy on itself, driven off course as it is by the assaults of the concurrent diversities of our world. In other words, 'rules' are made not by the old universal law, but by the accumulation of relations. This is obvious in the game of international politics today, where the law once again has to be defined, with difficulty, as we go along, and then supported by the pressure of monolithic armed forces opposing the action of the gradually diminishing forces of diversity. The establishment of these rights or of this new law is itself the sign of the nullification of the old universal law, which did not have to justify its 'quasi ontological' scope. The new law is only institutional, armed; it has to take into account this accumulation of relations, that is, it no longer plays tricks, or hides, and it hardly sublimates, unlike colonial oppression had done. In any case, the question of Being has been eliminated. What is coming to light here, beneath the spectacle of the hegemonies, is nothing other than the break-up of the generalizing universal, and, a priori, the surprise of the being, of the existent rising up, as against the permanence of Being.

All this is underpinned, in my view, by what I call trace thought. The trace presupposes and carries not the thought of Being but the ramblings of the existent. The progress of history is now barricaded by obscure turnings back, by what appear to be attempts to start again, whereby the peoples and communities that invented the idea of History churn up their uncertainties. They have confronted not only the other, the different, but, even more arduously, the turbulences of spatial extension ['l'étendue']. As we know, the single root claims the dimension of depth and the rhizomatic root extends horizontally outwards. The blank spaces on the maps of the planet are now criss-crossed with opacity, which has broken forever the absolute of History, which was above all project and projection. From now on, the concept of History is falling apart even as it rehashes these returns of the identitarian, the national, the fundamental, which are all the more sectarian now that they have become obsolete. As against these reversions to the old routes, the trace is the trembling thrust of that which is forever new. For what it opens up is not virgin land, virgin forest, that fierce passion of the discoverers. Indeed, it does not try to complete the totality; it enables us to conceive what the totality cannot express. The forever new is no longer that which still has to be discovered in order to complete the totality, that which still has to be discovered in the blank spaces on the map; rather, it is what still has to be undermined in order to fragment the totality – that is, ultimately, to accomplish it.

The trace is to the route as the revolt to the injunction and jubilation to the garrotte. It is not a rough sketch of the land, a babbling of the forest, but the organic inclination towards a different way of being and knowing; and it is the moving form of that knowledge. One does not follow the trace to rejoin comfortable paths, it is dedicated to its truth, which is to explode, to constantly chip away at the seductive norm. The Africans who were transported to the Americas carried with them over the Immense Waters the trace of their gods, their customs, their *langages*. Faced with the implacable disorder of the colonizer, they discovered within themselves, linked to the suffering they endured, a genius for fertilizing these traces: creating, better than syntheses, the new outcomes of which they had the secret. The Creole languages are traces opened up across the waters of the Caribbean and the Indian Ocean. When they became maroons in the woods, the traces they followed were not those of abandonment or despair, but nor were they those of pride or vanity. The proud Longoués, characters in one of my novels, *Le Quatrième Siècle*, could not get the better of the tenacious Béluses. The 'graine-en-bas-feuille',* a humble plant lost in the vegetation of my country, grew there as well as the proud 'porcelain rose', and this trace did not weigh on the land as an irreparable stigma. We all override in ourselves the traces of our offended histories; not in order to detour around a model of humanity that we would oppose, but around all the other patterns that we are forced to impose on ourselves. This is indeed the detour that is neither fleeing nor giving up, but the new art of freeing up the world.

The trace does not repeat the footpath that goes nowhere, where one stumbles, nor the well-kept avenue that ends with a territory, with the

---

* A medicinal plant used to treat fever, rheumatism, etc.

master's estate. It is an opaque way of experiencing the branch and the wind, of being oneself drifting towards the other, the sand in true utopian disorder, the unfathomed, the darkness of the current in the river set free. The Antillean landscapes urge on the others far away, and every folktale draws across them its winding, singular trace, from streams to rivers, establishing correlations; these fragile interconnected branches of *langages* call out to each other as they run and persist. Hills and valleys hurtle down in stories, crushing all that is unexplained in the world. Do not reject this new theme as it struggles, do not take offence at its insolent words, nor at those that you judged covered in too many lands, too much space. They proclaim the improbable and the risk that we share. Trace thought thus promises an alliance far from systems, it refuses possession, it gives onto these diffracted times that human beings today are multiplying between themselves, though conflicts and marvels.

Such is the violent wandering of the poem.

These literatures whose emergence I foresee, these literatures of the world, I think that they will be possible only if we affirm at their beginning – at the place we are in and from where we can guess at their emergence – that which I believe to be and which I call, in connection with the problems of identity, everyone's right to opacity.

In the planet-wide encounter of cultures, that we experience as chaos, it seems that we no longer have any landmarks. Everywhere we look, we find catastrophe and death throes. We despair of the chaos-world. But this is because we are still trying to discern in it a sovereign order that would once again bring the world-totality back to a reductive unity. Let us have the imaginative and utopian strength to realize that this chaos is not the apocalyptic chaos of the end of the world. Chaos is beautiful when one understands that all its elements are equally necessary. In the meeting up of all the world's cultures, we must have the imaginative strength to conceive of all the cultures as exerting an action of both liberating unity and liberating diversity. That is why I call for the right to opacity for everyone. I no longer have to 'understand' the other, that is, to reduce him to the model of my own transparency, in order to live with this other or to build something with him. Today, the right to opacity is the most obvious sign of non-barbarity. And I will say that the literatures that are beginning to appear in front of us and that we can foresee will be beautiful with all the illuminations and all the opacities of our world-totality.

QUESTIONS

Robert Melançon. I would like to start with an expression you quoted when you read the extracts of that very fine text, the Roma's appeal to you to come to Sarajevo: 'multi-ethnic democracy'. It is this word democracy that makes me want to ask you to extend your proposals a little further, into an area that is doubtless not your intention this evening, namely, the juridical and the political. It seems to me that the idea of citizenship in the world, the idea of citizenship as formulated by Locke for instance, and later as it was partially achieved in the French Revolution, this idea according to which there is no 'droit du sang'* but a right based rather on belonging and submitting to a set of laws – it seems to me that this idea of citizenship is being eroded somewhat throughout the world, that it is being undermined by all kinds of identitarian reflexes. It is quite clear almost everywhere how the 'droit du sol', which itself is not perfect, is under attack even in France from the 'droit du sang'. For this open, multicultural citizenship, this dispersed totality that you evoke, could one imagine a weak juridical or political framework: in other words, return in a different sense to what Marxism called the withering away of the state? Shouldn't we call, not for the withering away of the state, but the withering away of states? Shouldn't we dream of weak states, voluntary renunciations of state sovereignties … there are perhaps no other ways of realizing this dispersed totality on the juridical and political level (which, I know, is not the level you are concerned with)?

Édouard Glissant. I would like to make one point first of all. I think that to combat the expression 'droit du sang', the expression 'droit du sol' was the wrong choice. Because it still relies on the idea of a territory that a community establishes for itself, with its frontiers, and I think that idea is just as 'wrong' as the idea of the 'droit du sang'. I think we need, on the level you are talking about, to find another juridical formula, of common law or civil law, to replace the formula 'droit du sol'. I think this is just as limiting as the formula 'droit du sang', paradoxically.

Secondly, it seems to me that one cannot reflect on the notion of the state, on the level you have chosen, without having explored all the various

---

* The legal concepts of *droit du sang* and *droit du sol* refer to two bases on which citizenship can be claimed. In the first, the person's nationality is that of his or her parents, while in the second it derives from the national territory in which the person is born.

changes that the state has undergone in the cultures of the world. For example, in histories such as the history of China or of India – I am not of course talking about the Chinese empire, which is quite monolithic – there are ways of experiencing the state and the relations between civil society and the state that we have not yet taken into account. It seems to me that when we think about the relationship between civil society and the state, we always do so in the framework of the civil, legislative or international law of the West. And it seems to me that this is lacking something in terms of diversity or openness to the idea. That is why I hesitate to answer your question now, especially because many supporters of a society closed in on itself are also supporters of a weakening of the state. We see that in many countries of the world. In the first place, what kind of state are we talking about? We need to learn from elsewhere, get away from Western filiation. And also, is the weakening of the state an end in itself? That is to say: can't the weakening of the state go hand in hand with a coercive society? This is quite possible. So I would hesitate to answer the question, for these reasons. I would also hesitate to define what a multi-ethnic democracy could be. This is the position of the Roma, but the Roma are Westerners. They have suffered, but they have lived through the ups and downs of Western history. And for them democracy, with what they add to it (multi-ethnic, hybrid, creolized, etc.) can be – in my view, must be – an ideal, a goal in the framework of European societies. I don't know if it is valid for other types of society.

Joël Desrosiers. I would like to ask two questions. I'll be brief. I heard you talking on the radio this morning about those two authors, those two writers, Saint-John Perse and Faulkner. I am struck by two paradigms in your thought. The first is that of plants: the rhizome, the root. The second is the scientific paradigm: chaos theory, the world totality. My question concerns the fascination that Saint-John Perse himself had for science: for you, is science imaginary? When you talk about the imagination of the world, does that ultimately correspond to a background of scientific imagination? What relation do you see between figures of abstraction (chaos, invariants, etc.) and this new imagination?

É.G. What I believe is that there is a development of 'science' in general that concerns us from the point of view of the very question of identity. Western science at its moment of triumph, in other words when it had no doubts – either as to its future progress or its methods – claimed to be moving continuously, in depth, even despite dramatic revolutions in thought, towards a truth that would be the truth of matter itself and that sooner or later would provide the explanation of the universe, of the world. That was the claim of Western science. Up until the day that the revolutions of science itself showed, on the basis of Heisenberg's uncertainty principle, that perhaps one could never get 'to the bottom of the matter' – because Heisenberg says that in order to see particles one must expose them to light, and that when one exposes them to light one perhaps changes their nature, and certainly changes their speed and direction. This uncertainty principle has become one of the common places of contemporary thought. There is an opacity in matter that makes it impossible to get round or across. And it is from this moment onwards that Western science itself makes its own revolution and produces that part of science that has become the sciences of chaos, where one renounces equational linearity, that is, the claim to progress in depth (the single root ...) towards a truth that would be the truth of matter, and where one begins to say that we have to describe what is in its spatial extension, which is indescribable. We have to try to describe it without laying claim to an absolute of knowledge that we might attain. This evolution of science seems to me linked to the conception of Being and the being. In other words, triumphant science for me would be in line with the philosophy of Being, and the science that doubts, that retreats from its certainties and says that we must go round in circles, that we will no longer move in a linear fashion but circulate in spatial extension, would be in line with the unexpectedness of being. And that's why I am interested in this process. I am interested as a poet, I am not in any way a scientist. I make no claim to that. But it seems to me that a poet can understand this. He can understand this upheaval in Western science, which is in fact Science, since it is only in the West (whereas for example the Chinese have invented just about everything) that the notion of science has appeared and grown so strong ... but you also know that the sciences of chaos have an aesthetic relevance. It is quite normal that there should be a sort of attraction here ... I have been criticized for it actually, an article came out in France: 'Oh yes, Glissant and his chaos, chaos theory, you know?' It would have been very nice if it had been my theory. One can choose to ignore the chaos-world, but then one is inclined to literally reproduce its disorder, one tries to adopt its power, through delusional attempts to unleash it. Or in contrast one can approach it through imagination, decipher its opacity to escape from it perhaps, or at any rate to create a fragile but persistent trace across it.

J.D. Edward Said, in *Culture and Imperialism* – I don't know if it has been translated into French – states that Western literature, the Western canons, preceded and enabled, through their aesthetic, the exploration and the subjugation of the world. He claims that identities do not exist, that they are nothing but imaginary constructions. In your aesthetic, how do you react to this assertion?

É.G. I certainly share it. I would also make it more nuanced. It's true that in order to conquer the world, one had first to dream it. And that therefore, Western writers and poets could be the harbingers of colonization. We can all can cite them all, Chateaubriand, Conrad, etc. But there have also been – because the West is not monolithic – there have also been, in Western literatures, poets who, while they indeed dreamed the world, protested against its colonization: Rimbaud wrote 'Les Blancs arrivent' ['The Whites are coming']. And Césaire picks up the same motif in *Et les chiens se taisaient*: 'Les Blancs débarquent' ['The Whites are landing']. A poet like Victor Segalen, who was a military doctor and worked on an escort vessel, produces, invents, imagines and constructs a system of exoticist thought that actually combats all exoticism and all colonization. Therefore, things are not clear-cut: because for me Segalen is a revolutionary poet. Honour and respect to Segalen. He was the first to ask the question of the world's diversity, to fight against exoticism as a complacent form of colonization; and he was a doctor on a military ship.

In other words, there are no simple oppositions here. However, it is true that traditional literature in the West is a literature of Being and of the absolute and so tends towards generalization. English and French colonization, the forms of English and French colonization which were dominant in the nineteenth century, are the only ones that that are absolutely sure of their legitimacy, absolutely. Today, whichever country colonizes or oppresses another country is not sure of its legitimacy. Let us suppose that a great power like China, Russia, the United States or Japan invades another country today: that power will not be sure of its legitimacy. It will have to explain it. French and English colonizations in the nineteenth century were sure of their legitimacy because it was the whole system (the idea of the chosen territory) that was expanding to the dimension of the world. And when the world was realized by colonization (the colonizers were its harbingers; it was they who discovered its coastlines, who made the maps, etc.), when all of that was 'realized', the legitimacy collapsed, because it could not extend any further. Rather like when people say that some of the American pioneers heading west, once they got to the Californian coast and couldn't go any further, thought about committing suicide. There was a kind of generalized depression. Expansion, forging ahead, was no longer possible. And I think that happened with the Western colonizations, and particularly the French and English ones. They were fought by the peoples they encountered, but they were also depressed by a loss of legitimacy. That is the nuance I would add to what you have told me about Said's position.

Gaston Miron. Right at the end, you said: 'To conceive of all cultures ... opacity' ... I didn't get the whole of the sentence. Could you re-read that passage?

É.G. Oh, yes: 'In the meeting up of all the world's cultures, we must have the imaginative strength to conceive of all the cultures as exerting an action of both liberating unity and liberating diversity'. But we don't have the imaginative strength to see it. And we must have that strength. We must have it ...

Pierre Nepveu. I have a question on the epic. When you dream of that literature that is coming, whose emergence you can feel, you talk about a new epic. I am slightly surprised by that characterization, in two ways. Firstly, can't we say that this new epic you refer to already exists in Western literature – starting with Joyce, obviously, but also very much in Latin American literature, for example in Fuentes, in Marquez, in Guimarães Rosa in Brazil – where we see the epic form re-used, certainly, but also unravelling at the same time, very often in a form of creolization of the *langage* or else references to everyday life (parody, etc.)? Secondly, could one not also say that what is happening in literature today is characterized by the end of any kind of epic model? If we look at the novel for instance, in some European writers there is a real rejection of the epic form, in order to open up the novel form to something else, which is played out in relation to music, in relation to the everyday, to intimacy, etc. There are all kinds of ways. It's as though there two different sides ... In other words, what is the reason for this very strong promotion of the epic, even in its new form?

É.G. It's not the epic as such, it's the epic form; the epic form can be realized in ways other than the epic as such. I'll reply to both questions. Your first objection: of course there are already appearances, re-appearances, of the epic form in Caribbean and Latin-American literatures. But these are epic forms that in my opinion remain within the traditional structure of the epic. That is to say, a community reassuring itself by the production of an epic that concerns only the members of that community. So, what is happening is that all the peoples who are decolonizing – and that includes the Latin-Americans and the Caribbeans – counter the Western epic with their own epic, which is very beautiful. But from my point of view it is still not the true epic, because the true epic has as its object the most threatened community in the world today, which is the world-community. And it is the relation between my community and the world-community that could be the basis for the epic. It seems to me that that the other literatures you have mentioned, which remain outside this problem, do not know the world and are not interested in the world, except perhaps to try again to rule it through the Narrative. That is their 'legitimacy'. It is not surprising that they renounce the epic voice, which today proclaims the splitting up, the dispersal of the Narrative and, against History, the meeting together, finally, of the histories of peoples.

✦ 4 ✦

The Chaos-world:
Towards an Aesthetic of Relation

I have chosen to speak to you about what I call 'the poetics of chaos', because it seemed to me a theme that would bring together and perhaps reach a provisional conclusion concerning what I have said about creolization and about language. I must admit that one cannot think about what I call the poetics of chaos in formal completion, that is, by means of a written, radical lecture with no possibility of revisions or contradictions. Nor can one think about these poetics of chaos in real completion, that is, as a whole that does not admit of additions, retreats, or even remorse or rejection. This is why I have chosen to make this presentation practically with you by dreaming about my subject, because it is a subject on which one can dream, construct, elaborate, conceptualize and also 'poetize'. The book that will be my starting point for exploring what I call the poetics of chaos is a book called *Des Rythmes au chaos*, published by Editions Odile Jacob, and written by Pierre Bergé, Yves Pomeau and Monique Dubois-Gance. It is a popularizing book that is perfectly accessible, but this popularization has the merit of being done by three specialists. In other words they are not just popularizers of science, they are specialists in the field who have written a work of popularization. I will spare you the list of works on chaos in the scientific sense of the term. I don't think that is the object of this discussion. Moreover, at one point the book's authors regret that people refer to chaos in the scientific sense in order to talk about anything and everything, and that they paraphilosophize around it. This is something I willingly lapse into. And elsewhere in the book, fortunately, they point out that the theories of chaos are theories of the philosophy of science and that these theories are pretty ambiguous; we will see the value of that ambiguity. I feel myself fully authorized – from my first prose work *Soleil de la conscience* right up to *Poétique de la Relation* I have engaged, for myself and for what concerns me, with the problematic of the chaos-world – to paraphilosophize around the science of chaos.

As I have said several times in the course of these lectures, I call chaos-world the shock, the intertwining, the repulsions, attractions, complicities, oppositions and conflicts between the cultures of peoples in the contemporary world-totality. Consequently the definition or, let's say, the approach that I propose for this notion of the chaos-world is quite precise: it is a cultural mixing, that is not a simple melting pot, whereby the world-totality today finds its realization. My first evaluation of it will highlight what we could call a temporal condition of culture, a temporal condition of the relation between cultures. The most general statement that one can make in this area is that the relations, the contacts between cultures – I've already said this elsewhere but I must repeat it – used to perpetuate themselves across huge expanses of time. These contacts, therefore, although very efficient and very effective, were not recognized as such. That is, the temporal expanse was so long that before the transformation – which is usually quite brutal and immediate – was perceived as such, it had been overtaken by another transformation. For instance, it took some time before the inhabitants of what would become France thought of themselves as French. There are these huge expanses of time that condition and contain the relations between cultures, and we study them mostly in the European world, because this is what we have been taught most about and, unfortunately, we are not only ignorant but also handicapped as regards knowledge of cultural relations in continents such as Asia or Africa. Nevertheless we know that in these huge expanses of time cultures imperceptibly influence one another, but with transformations that are sometimes quite dazzling. What is new about our contemporary times is that the temporal expanses are no longer huge, they are immediate, and the impact is immediate. The influences or impacts of cultures on one another are immediately felt as such. And at the same time as there is this immediacy of the impact of cultural relations, of cultures on one another, there is also an observation that one cannot avoid making, namely that the human communities who are thus influencing each other, in negative or positive ways, are living several different times. Compared with the measure that we have, which is the historical measure manifested by the linearity of Western time before and after Jesus Christ, one can say that the cultures of our period are living several different times but undergo the same transformations, or the same influences. In other words there is a kind of contraction, of fracture, of sharp contradiction in the fact that cultures which live different times are subject to the same influences. A Chinese peasant who has lived for thousands of years in a very long space-time undergoes or experiences in a brutal way the Chinese Revolution for example, while at the same time he is affected by the influence of, the desire for, Coca-Cola; the same Coca-Cola that is experienced quite differently in New York or Miami or London. There are fractures or contradictions on that level, which lead us immediately to a principal element of the science of chaos: the notion of an erratic deterministic system. I can't 'do science' with you, I am absolutely no good at that, but the notion of an erratic deterministic system, which is one of the basic notions of chaos theory in physics, is applicable to what I call the chaos-world.

Chaos theory says that there are determined dynamic systems that become erratic. In principle, a deterministic system has a fixity, a mechanical quality and a regularity in its functioning; the discovery of chaos theory is that there are an infinite number of determined dynamic systems that become erratic, that is to say – as I interpret it – whose system of values at a certain moment begins to waver for no apparent reason. The scientists of chaos test this notion of the erratic deterministic system that they verify in a whole series of aspects and representations of the real. For example, in the unpredictable movement of leaves falling in the wind or in the winter rain, or the fundamental impossibility of defining the exact length of the coast of Brittany. Chaos theory says that we can absolutely not define the exact length of the coast of Brittany because we cannot control the fluctuation of the coast at the border between the water and the land, and the turmoil of the coast opens up a strangeness that cannot be fixed once and for all. I don't want to use this as any kind of bible, but something about it interests me, in the context of the human cultures of today. And what interests me is the unpredictable behaviour of this relation between cultures, an unpredictability that is one of the bases of chaos theory. Unpredictable behaviour is linked to the notion of an erratic deterministic system. The physicists of chaos say that any system which has only two degrees of freedom, in other words two variables, never becomes erratic. But that beyond that, when the variables multiply and especially when one introduces the variable of time – this is why I started this little exposition with time – then unpredictability is confirmed. And what I am saying is that the relations between the world's cultures, today, are unpredictable. We have lived for a long time under the pressure and the precious teaching of the West, in systematic thought whose main ambition was predictability. All systematic thought aims at predictability. And we see that as regards the relations of cultures, that is, those space-times that communities secrete around themselves and fill with projects, concepts and often inhibitions, unpredictability rules. Here I think we should pause for a second and ask this: if unpredictability rules as regards the mutual relations of the cultures of human communities, are we not going to fall into completely destructive pessimism or nihilism? That is no doubt what systematic thought wanted to avoid: that the density of the unpredictability would lead human cultures to give up, to stagnate – if it's unpredictable, why act and why create? We will have to respond to this question.

The other idea I want to follow up is that one of the principles of the erratic nature of certain deterministic systems stems from the fact that these systems are sensitive to their initial conditions. This sensitivity means that sometimes an over- or underestimate in the evaluation of the initial conditions can multiply infinitely and erratically within the system. This idea greatly interested me because I saw in it another idea that I have formulated: the *prophetic vision of the past*. The past must not only be reconstructed objectively (or even subjectively) by the historian, it must also be dreamed prophetically, for those people, communities and cultures whose past has actually been hidden from them. For instance, I remember – this anecdote has always amused me – that in a novel called *Le Quatrième siècle*, I had imagined the giving of names to slaves who had no names at the liberation from slavery in Martinique in 1848. I had imagined the scene where two French clerks, lost in a crowd of Blacks, gave people and families names, authoritatively handed out surnames, and they had books beside them, encyclopaedias or collections of texts, etc. So they named families Cicero, Cato, Caesar, etc., and then the Oats family, the Wheat family, etc., and then the Trade Wind family, the Elysée family, etc. They exhausted the whole of Western knowledge to give names to the newly liberated slaves. And sometime later, I found in an extremely serious, exclusive and very scientific journal about the origin of names – what do you call it … the origin of proper names … onomastics, that's it – in a very specialized onomastic journal, I found a text written by an expert in the subject which took as its reference point on the question that chapter from *Le Quatrième siècle* that I had totally imagined and totally invented, and that chapter became an element of scientific illustration. It was a prophetic vision of the past. In other words, there are concealed phenomena in human cultures that can produce substantive variants which sometimes escape analysis. If we really want to study poverty in Africa – not study, that really would be the limit if we 'studied' Africa's poverty – if we want to understand the poverty-stricken and disturbing reality of Africa today (and even so without succumbing to any 'Afro-pessimism'), how could we do so without that sensitivity to initial conditions that is the memory of the horrible holocaust of the slave trade, the depopulation and devastation of Africa for three centuries? How could we do it? The erratic system that the African continent has become cannot be understood without going back to that sensitivity, that initial condition that is the horrible holocaust of the slave trade through the centuries.

The current poverty in Haiti and the kind of complacent ambiguity that exists in Martinique, two completely opposite poles, both result from that same initial condition: transportation and the violent seizing of the populations of Africa. What I want to try and share with you is my conviction that thought systems or systematic thought no longer give us any contact with the real, no longer provide the understanding or the means to assess what is really happening in the contacts and conflicts of culture. Because the erratic, the erratic dimension that is the dimension of determinist systems with multiple variables, according to chaos theory, the erratic dimension has become the dimension of the 'Whole-World'. Today's wanderings no longer aim to found a territory. A territory is variable in its dimensions, but it is not erratic. The fixity of the territory is terrifying.

For a very long time – one must always repeat this – for a very long time, Western wandering, which was all about conquest and founding territories, contributed to the realization of what we can today call the 'world-totality'. But in the same space in which today there are more and more internal wanderings – that is to say, more and more projections towards the world-totality and retreats into oneself while remaining immobile, without moving from one's own place – these forms of wandering often result in what one calls internal exile, that is, moments when imagination or sensibility are cut off from what is happening around one. Yes, internal exile. The erratic nature of the Whole-World, the absolutely unpredictable character of the relation between the cultures of human communities today, has, whether one is aware of it or not, an impact on the mentality or the reactive capacity of one or several members of a community. What maintains the wandering is a kind of general coming together in a cultural place, experienced as acceptance or as suffering. And it is one of the givens of the chaos-world that acceptance of one's surroundings or suffering in one's surroundings are equally valid as pathways and means of knowing one's surroundings. And that consequently the negativity of suffering is just as much a constituent of identity as spontaneous, joyful or victorious acceptance. We are in the presence of systems of relations which are completely erratic systems. And what makes the Whole-World is not cosmopolitanism, absolutely not cosmopolitanism, which is a negative version of Relation. What makes the Whole-World is the actual poetics of this Relation which allows one to sublimate, through knowledge of the self and the whole, both suffering and acceptance, the negative and the positive.

These considerations allow me to return to the ideas of creolization and hybridity. Oversimplifying drastically: hybridity is determinism and creolization, compared to hybridity, is the producer of unpredictability. Creolization is the unpredictable. One can predict or control hybridity, one cannot predict or control creolization. The same idea of ambiguity that the specialists of chaos theory observe at the base of their discipline now governs the imagination of the chaos-world and of Relation. This can be summed up in the opposition between archipelagic thought and continental thought, the latter being systematic thought and the former ambiguous thought.

At this point in our reasoning, we must ask ourselves the question: does unpredictability constitute a deficiency? We agree of course that the predictability of systems of thought has not been particularly effective or positive for the development of human communities. But is unpredictability not a deficiency, or does it not at least open onto a deficiency of will-power, of the will, or what Schopenhauer called the will to live? Given that simple deterministic systems cannot be chaotic, with negative effects, doesn't this system – if we consider the world as a deterministic system – doesn't this manifestly erratic deterministic system perhaps lead to a deterioration of being? My answer to this question is that to know the unpredictable is to shape oneself to one's present, the present time that one is living, in a different way, no longer empirical, no longer systematic, but poetic. People in France say that poetry is dead. I believe that poetry, or in any case the exercise of the imagination, the prophetic vision both of the past and of distant regions, is the only way we have of placing ourselves in the unpredictability of the world-wide relation.

No global operation on the level of politics, economics or military intervention is capable of even beginning to glimpse the slightest solution to the contradictions of this erratic system that constitutes the chaos-world unless the imagination of Relation impacts on the mentalities and sensibilities of human communities today to push them into reversing the direction of poetics, that is, to conceive of themselves, human communities and not Humanity, in a different way: as rhizome rather than single root. I think no intervention in Burundi, or Rwanda, or Yugoslavia, or any other place in the world is capable of 'resolving' the situation until the mentalities of human communities have changed on this point: that our existences and our influences on each other are characterized by unpredictability. As long as we go on living with the idea of identity as single root, there will be more Bosnias, more Rwandas, more Burundis, and each time we will find ourselves facing the same impossibility. When I was talking with Tutsi friends in Rwanda I was absolutely convinced that they were the victims of a Hutu plot; but I am also sure that if there were five hundred Tutsis and ten Hutus, the ten Hutus would be dead. And if there were five hundred Hutus and ten Tutsis, the ten Tutsis would be dead. In other words, there is no solution. There is no solution within the identitarian framework of systematic thought. Neither in the appeal for tolerance (or pity), which is the luxury of systematic thought, nor by recourse to force. And when I am told that in Yugoslavia it's the Bosnians who are in the wrong, it's the Serbs who are in the wrong, it's the Croatian Muslims who are in the wrong, it's these people or those people who are in the wrong, we return to the old intransigence and we choose our victims, we choose our executioners according to whose side we are on, and we go back to all the useless talk. One must never hesitate to defend the oppressed and the victim, but the problem is to change the very idea, the very depth of the way we live our identity, and to realize that only the imagination of the Whole-World (that is, the fact that I can live in my own place while being in relation with the world-totality), only that imagination can enable us to go beyond these sorts of fundamental limits that no-one wishes to go beyond. The Whole-World exceeds all measure, and if we do not take the measure of this immeasurability ['démesure'] we risk – this is one of the reference points of my poetics, of what one could call my poetics – dragging with us for ever and ever the old impossibilities that always cause intolerance, massacres and genocides.

We must take the measure–immeasurability of the prophetic vision of the past and of the imagination of Relation, with its treatment of the initial conditions and its traces of the initial conditions, with its unpredictability and with this new tissue that we must create, which is no longer the reflection of an essence but the network of connections, of the connection with the other and the connections with other cultures. The Whole-World exceeds all measure.

What I would like to suggest to you now, to finish, is neither a set of instructions nor a kind of catalogue. Rather, I dream of a new approach, a new appreciation of literature, of literature as the discovery of the world, as discovery of the Whole-World. I believe that all peoples today have an important role to fulfil in the Whole-World's non-system of relations, and that a people that lacks the means to reflect on this function is indeed an oppressed people, a people kept in a state of weakness. And then I dream, for myself, since I am a writer, I dream of a new approach to literature in this reality beyond measure that is the Whole-World.

(Technical advances, achieved by the industrial countries and securing their privilege in the world, both speed up and slow down the diversity of the Whole-World. The internet for example and the other 'information highways' make possible a multi-relation that opens diversity up to infinity. But the advances in these areas also lead to a sort of non-reality, as for example the 'virtual realities' in the domain of computer science. This is perhaps a flight response, faced with all the anxiety caused by the complexities of the Whole-World. Whatever its advantages, virtual reality is no more effective in the human imagination than a universal Esperanto would be in the area of language and expression.)

Dreaming of contemporary literature. I will take the example of French literature, but I think one could choose a quite different one. I will start with what I call a measure of measure. Why? Because the measure of measure is always a classicism. *Measure* of measure, this *measure* is of course metric measure. Whether it is classical measure, Latin or Greek or French or Italian, it is metric measure. Measure of *measure*: this measure is the original breath, that is, the measure that exists in our voice, our breath and our ability to speak continuously without running out of breath. We will see later that this is for example the measure of the stanza. The stanza, the breath that we emit without running out of breath, in a single 'burst'. Why then this measure of the measure? Because every classicism addresses the world. And why does it address the world? Because, in this measure of the measure, every classicism claims to make the world adopt its particular values as universal values. For a given culture, classicism represents the moment when that culture is sufficiently sure of its own values to inscribe them in this measure of measure and offer them to the world as universal values. This is where I start from. Before this, there are of course all the cultural accumulations of the community, for example the creation of new words by Ronsard and the Pléiade, the definition of cultural relativism by Montaigne, Rabelais's testing of educational systems and heretical turning of things upside down. All these accumulations work towards a moment

– calling them accumulations does not mean that they are 'inferior', but makes the point that literature here has a different function, which is to dig cultures over, to pick up earth, pick up compost, pick up fertile works, etc. – to come finally to that measure of measure that is classicism, which proposes its particular values to the world as universal values.

We know that in all the world's cultures, classicisms are followed by baroque periods. And that in these baroque periods there develops an immeasurability of measure. The baroque in Western cultures (in France the eighteenth-century libertines, Cyrano de Bergerac, Saint-Amant, etc.), at the very moment at which the classical ambition is fulfilled, introduces that *immeasurability* of measure which comes to stand for the opposite of the classical ambition. A denial. This *immeasurability* is a denial of metric measure. In other words, the function of the baroque is to oppose the classical ambition and the claims it makes. And the classical claim is of course that of *depth*. If I propose to the world my particular values as universal values, it means I believe that I have achieved depth. And, of course, the baroque is spatial *extension*. The baroque is extension, that is, the renouncing of the claim to depth. It is well known that all the baroque arts – architecture, painting or literature – are the arts of extension, of proliferation, redundancy and repetition.

This period is followed by another that I will call the measure of immeasurability. This measure is once again the original breath, but this immeasurability is not that of the metrical measure, but of the world: it is the immeasurability of the world. And its claim is to express through the original breath the immeasurability of the world – this is Claudel, it's Saint-John Perse, and of course before them it's Segalen. What is going on here is a process of learning about the world, about the ongoing immeasurability of the world. A learning process, but in a centred mode, that is, the original breath comes from a centre and extends to its peripheries. Hence the importance of the stanza, which is not a metre but a mastering. Man's breath measuring the immeasurability of the world.

And this is followed in turn by what I call an immeasurability of immeasurability, which seems to me to be the vocation of today's literature. Immeasurability not because it is anarchic, but because there is no longer the claim of depth, the claim of universality, there is now only the claim to diversity. *Immeasurability* of immeasurability. The first *immeasurability* is total openness and the second is the Whole-World. Literature has followed this path. And it is quite obvious that the francophone literatures are situated here, in the immeasurability of immeasurability. And that they do not have to claim the denial operated by the baroque, nor the depth of classicism, because they are living the diversity and the immeasurability of the Whole-World. If I was a scholar I would say that I have gone from the measure of measure to the immeasurability of measure, to the measure of immeasurability and then the immeasurability of immeasurability, and that I have made a chiasmus. MM, IM, MI, II. I have made a chiasmus. Not everyone can make a chiasmus. But it can be done with the literature of the Whole-World!

I wanted to draw up this incomprehensible little diagram for you, to make you dream. Dream of the state and the current situation of literature, truly. And because I believe that literature can be beautiful, to quote Henri Pichette, only if it is embedded in the world. And I believe that my identity and my problems can only be tackled and harmonized, for myself and others, if I put them in the context of the immeasurability of the Whole-World and the goal that this immeasurability is now proposing for literature. And I think that it is only through this new way of conceiving the literary object that we can escape from the old fixities, the old imprisonments, from everything that has trained us, that has made us – as countries, real, concrete countries, and as intellectuals, artists, writers and poets of the South – try to free ourselves in the name of the very principles that have been imposed on us, without ever challenging these. To challenge the principles is perhaps to struggle and to dream. I do not believe that struggle and dreaming are contradictory.

QUESTIONS

Robert Melançon. You started by evoking two types of time … explaining that the contacts which used to take place across very large expanses of time have given way today to contacts which are formed in extremely limited temporal spaces. You spoke of an immediate impact. I want to ask my question in two ways. First, even if the contacts are now made in very restricted temporal expanses, in which events that were previously spaced out are now compressed, this does not abolish the long-term perspective. We don't know what is waiting for us in the very long-term future that stretches out in front of us. And on the other hand, it seems to me that at the end, towards the end, you cannot help getting involved in the problems of the long term. When you referred to the unpredictability of the chaos-world, you contrasted its unpredictable character with systematic thought, and you said: no intervention in Burundi or Bosnia or anywhere else will be productive as long as the mentalities have not changed, as long as we have not moved on from systematic thought. Mentalities have a very slow evolution: this does not prevent the immediate impact of cultures on one another in this chaos-world that we live in ... but it nor does it negate the fact that mentalities continue to change at a very slow speed.

Édouard Glissant. Yes, but the difference is that we know this. It's an important difference. The consciousness of consciousness is a decisive factor. The huge expanse of time is not so much a question of time as a question of non-consciousness, that is, not of unawareness but of non-knowledge of the situation. That's what the huge expanse of time actually is. It's the non-knowledge of the situation. Whatever the difficulties, however long it takes, however slowly it proceeds, the fundamental difference in the relations between cultures today – the important point is that we are aware of it. The very concept of knowledge of the relations, the phenomena of relations between cultures, produces immediacy. It may be a distorted knowledge, as with the knowledge that comes from television or radio for instance. Perhaps not a true knowledge, a para- or a pseudo-knowledge, but the phenomenon of knowledge intervenes immediately, which is not the case in these huge expanses of time that we have talked about, and that is the great difference, in my view. For example, unpredictability is only negative when it is not known. That is, when one has the vanity to prepare for or protect oneself against the future, on the basis of predictability. That is where unpredictability is negative. But when one is in harmony with unpredictability, in one's imagination, one can avoid the non-responsibility that it produces.

R.M. Hasn't the abolition of the temporal expanses, precisely, led to a flattening out of cultural and linguistic variations, and the uniformization of the Whole-World rather than its diversity?

É.G. I don't think so. Because, for creolization and relation to exist, there have to be different cultural values. Segalen himself says that there is a kind of opposition there, which is beneficial. Rather like Valéry, who claimed that the resistance posed by regular metre refines the poet's sensibility. Well, standardization cannot be a mode of the Whole-World. Standardization and banalization cannot be modes of the Whole-World. For there to be a relation, there have to be different terms. That is why, in modern times, we have attached so much importance to the notion of difference. Because if there are no differences, there is no relation. For instance, a people that has been assimilated into another people cannot participate in world-wide relation. For it to do so, it has to put up a resistance to the process of assimilation attempted by the other people. But if it puts up this resistance by being closed in on itself, and this is the crucial point, then it is doing the same thing, neither more nor less, than its oppressor. It does not enter into the world-wide relation. But, in my opinion, diversity is not a melting pot, a mush, a mish-mash, etc. Diversity means differences that encounter each other, adjust, clash, harmonize and produce something unforeseeable. Standardization is certainly a danger, but the whole idea of the Whole-World helps to combat this danger.

Joël Desrosiers. This is about your question on creolization. I will formulate mine in the same way, as a commentary: fluidity between cultures, hybridity between cultures, is a primary given, fundamental, based first of all on biology, and Segalen as a doctor was very aware of this (Éloge du divers).* Purity and the single root have only ever existed in the passion surrounding identity, in other words, ideologically. So it seems to me that creolization, understood here as an impurity, in fact summons up the idea of purity, as the antithesis presupposes its thesis. Could we dream – since you've made me dream – of something beyond creolization, beyond identity?

É.G. We are at a moment in the world-totality where we are beginning to escape from the strait-jackets and imprisonments of identity as the single root. We are beginning to conceive of it. When one reads history, when one reads about the current state of the world, one can see this everywhere. And it's the question that no-one wants to risk asking, that no-one wants to hear about. Because if one asks this question, one feels as though one is mutilating or amputating one's own identity; so, no-one 'wants' creolization. Because one can die for one's single root-identity, but one cannot die for creolization. Creolization demands that one does not die. (Even though Segalen asked, against the decline of the Diverse in the world, that we should struggle, fight, 'perhaps die with beauty'.) One cannot sacrifice oneself for creolization, whereas one can sacrifice oneself for one's identity: for one's single root-identity, etc. One can become an

---

* *Eloge du divers* does not in fact exist; Glissant is probably thinking of Segalen's *Essai sur l'exotisme*.

assassin, a murderer, a butcher for one's single root-identity. One can make war for one's single root-identity. So, when I start in my imagination to think of Relation as constitutive of my being, am I not starting to separate myself from my being, to weaken my identity, to vanish into thin air? No. Until we effect this reversal, Bosnias will still happen. To go beyond creolization would in fact be to go beyond identity. But there is still the Place, which supports us.

J.D. I wonder if it is always easy to identify who are the colonizers and who are the colonized. For instance in Quebec, are the partisans of sovereignty in fact the colonizers?

É.G. That's for the Quebeckers to answer. I am going to be 'diplomatically' careful because I have many friends in Quebec. In any case, I can say this: I never intervene in the way in which people work out their connection to their place. One cannot work out the connection to a place on behalf of the people who live there. But if I was a Quebecker, and a fiercely nationalist Quebecker, I would also be a fiercely nationalist Amerindian, I would be fiercely nationalist for the Amerindians. If I was a fiercely nationalist Quebecker … Because just as one cannot save one particular language while letting the others perish, one can also not save a nation or an ethnicity while leaving the others to waste away. And that's what I call Relation.

Gaston Miron. Canada would not allow one to be a fiercely nationalist Amerindian because that would upset the whole strategy for the Indian nations.

É.G. But we have to upset strategies! The Indian peoples are 'atavistic' peoples, let's not forget that. And, whatever they think about it themselves, the Quebeckers are a composite people compared with the atavistic Amerindian peoples. It will be more difficult for an atavistic people to accept Relation. Especially since they have suffered from the situation. It is easier to accept Relation when one is Brazilian rather than when one is a Quechua or a descendant of the Hurons, because in their case there is the weight of atavism countering the dispersal of the composite. There is the weight of extreme suffering and dispossession. Until these peoples consent freely to Relation, it will be under threat.

In addition, the appearance of the real obliterates the traces of the initial conditions underneath. And we often lose this trace of the initial conditions. We can look at a culture that really dominates another one, and we can think that it does not dominate it. A people that physically oppresses another one, and we can think that it dominates it culturally, and it's not true. Relation contains all possibilities because it is an erratic deterministic system, not a mechanical deterministic system. And, what can seem to be colonialist can in reality not be so, and vice versa. We must overturn the principles!

G.M. I feel that you are investing a lot of hopes in literature to create a new imagination and perhaps eventually a new world order, which would be that of creolization. Is this not rather utopian?

É.G. Absolutely, it is utopian. But I think that nothing worthwhile can be done on earth without utopia. I don't know of any great work achieved by human communities without utopia.

G.M. Do you think that literature could be capable of leading to a new kind of behaviour?

É.G. Yes, I do. Literature in the sense of Narrative, which is History's witness, and as it were the unknown privilege of those who 'made' History, that literature is sterile. But the passion and the poetics of the world-totality can show the way to a new relationship to Place and flush out, change, the old reflexes.

G.M. I was just taking notes, which shows how interested I am. You said: a people that cannot reflect on something or other – that's the bit I didn't catch – is a people that …

É.G. A people that cannot reflect on its function in the world is indeed an oppressed people. True liberation for a people in the Whole-World today means being able to reflect and act on its function in the world. If it can't, that is no good, it means it is still dominated and oppressed.

G.M. Can you first of all go back over what you mean by a poetic vision of the world? And then, can you expand on this link between unpredictability and the poetic vision of the world?

É.G. I first asked the question: doesn't unpredictability entail a loss of the will to live, or to create meaning, or to express oneself? Unpredictability has always frightened cultures, particularly in the West, perhaps less so in the rest of the world. Western cultures have always tended towards predictability, that is to say: to drawing up ambitious plans – social plans, political plans, etc. And giving that up is perhaps frightening for the way we think. It can be frightening to give up on the ability to 'change the world'. Because to change the world means this, it means giving the world a future, that is, predicting. And giving that up is perhaps frightening for our sensibility. What is the point of being in the world and living if one cannot at least predict that it is going to work? I think that predictability has known some excesses. In other words, the noble formula 'changing the world' has gradually been transformed into 'mapping out the world, systematizing it'. So I say that poetic vision enables us to live with the idea of unpredictability because it allows us to think of unpredictability not as a negative but as a positive, and it enables us to change our sensibility on this issue whereas no concept or conceptual system could do so. That is to say, a poetic intention can enable me to conceive that in my relation to the other, to others, to all the others, to the world-totality, I change myself through exchanging with the other, while remaining myself, without rejecting myself, without diluting myself, and one needs nothing less than a poetics to conceive of these impossibilities. That's why I think that poetic thought today is at the core of our relation to the world.

G.M. Isn't the single root in the process of disappearing in some sense in some very specific places, because today it's economic rationality that is in charge (the globalization of the economy, of markets, of production, of consumption, everyone in the universe must wear the same jeans, etc., because of economies of scale, etc.)? I was listening to an international discussion where there were several representatives of many peoples, of nations if you like, of countries, I don't know what to call them … And they were all enslaved to the laws of the market. And there was no longer any single root, or whatever else, values, imagination, etc. It was a total enslavement. Whatever the language or culture, everything was sacrificed to the laws of the market. They said: 'But we can't do anything, it's the laws of the market. We have to abide by the laws of the market. And so we have to melt into a kind of great universal economic rationality.'

É.G. The economy has become globalized, just as political life has become globalized, as knowledge of the culinary arts has become globalized, as literature has become globalized. We are living this globalization because we are faced with, we are in, the world-totality. The problem is that in the period when literatures were the literatures of classicism – in other words they proposed their particular values as universal, the value of one place as a universal value – the economic oppressions were of the same style. That is, it was the economy of Britain or France or some other country that dominated and oppressed the world. Today, with globalization, it is not just the economy of the United States or Canada that oppresses us, it is the multinationals, that is to say people, circles whose circumference is everywhere and their centre nowhere. In other words, if we fall back on our old reactions, let's say of national citizens, we go the wrong way about reacting to these people. Because they don't give a damn about national citizens. In other words we must immerse ourselves in the idea of globalization, in all the areas of our activities. We must immerse ourselves in this idea, or else we will rapidly become obsolete in relation to people who will exploit the possibilities of globalization in negative and malicious ways. We must be conscious of globalization. Otherwise no-one will be able to fight these people. In the first place one cannot fight them physically, because the multinationals are invisible. You can't fight. You could struggle physically against the King of France, who was the representative of French capitalism. Against the colonizer. Against the Boss. But you cannot struggle physically, I say physically, against the multinationals. (Except in a quite factual way, for instance when they make themselves visible in ecological damage.) Where can you find them? None of us here has the slightest little idea of the real location of the slightest little multinational. Because the multinationals are the negative aspect of globalization. If we refuse to conceive of this globalization, we will be its unconscious victims. Moreover, we must not go on having the same old reflexes. We will stagnate if we stick to the old principles that the Western 'powers' instilled in us, in other words that the collectivity's existence is demonstrated by its power, precisely. We dream of 'great' countries. Whereas no-one can claim to be an unavoidable power, because in unpredictability even powers are fragile. Economic systems are powerful and implacable, but also vulnerable to the unpredictability of the totality.

G.M. Do you think that that there is perhaps a certain ambivalence between the literary production of *créolité*,* where there is a certain quest for a unique identity, if one can put it like that – I'm thinking of Chamoiseau and Confiant – and the project of *créolité* as they define it in Éloge de la créolité, where there is in fact a certain quest for the world-totality, a totality first of the Caribbean and then of the world?

É.G. There is a difference, yes, between creative works and manifestos. But I think that it is in literary works, and not in theoretical projects, that the approach to the world-totality first takes shape. But having said that, I don't myself see the contradiction to which you refer. I don't think that these writers are in search of the 'single root'.

Joël Desrosiers. Identity, never mind how one analyses it or summarizes it, has a function as a direction and a means for the society, a political function. You said so a moment ago. One can even die for a flag, die for an identity. It has a political function. The American Negro today declares himself a *Black* African-American; that has a political function. When literature becomes – as you define it, as you emphasize today – an almost post-national literature, not unlike the multinationals, what happens to that identity now? That is, how does it affect political reality?

É.G. First of all, I have always said: place is crucial. There is no globalization on the basis of a series of dilutions into thin air. Because if there is dilution, there is no relation. Relation can weave itself only between entities that continue to exist. The more I am conscious of the relation between Martinique and the Caribbean and between the Caribbean and the world, as in a system, in a non-system of relations, the more I will be Martiniquan, I think. The more I say: Martinique is Martinique, the others are … the less I will be Martiniquan, I think. The true relation is not from the particular to the universal, but from the Place to the world-totality, which is not totalitarian but the opposite: diversity. The place is not a territory: we agree to share the place, we think of it and experience it in the thinking of wandering, even while defending it against any kind of damage.

The Blacks in the United States do of course need Afro-centrism to struggle against their condition and one cannot ask a black homeless

---

* The *créolité* 'movement', which seeks to promote Creole culture and identity, is associated with Patrick Chamoiseau, Raphaël Confiant and Jean Bernabé.

person in New York to rise up in the name of creolization. Just as there are countries (Panama, Brazil, Columbia) where Negritude is dominant. The connection of these communities to the Americas and to the world is nevertheless made through creolization, which it becomes profitable to explore in order to better understand one's own richness. So, that is my first response. The second is that I now believe that we are working in a framework in which literature is becoming oral – on the one hand because various kinds of collective oral poetry are developing; on the other hand because the techniques of writing are becoming 'oralized', and I'm not talking about the banalized orality of television or the media, I'm talking about a creative use of oral expression. Here, ideas, in my view, are being diffused in a way that is no longer the sensationalist diffusion of the television and the media, but the real diffusion of a change of imagination. And I think that this is the important thing. The means, the elements of echo, of feedback, of multiplication and proliferation, are changing. And paradoxically, there is a sort of neutralization by what I call the 'splash' function of television and newspapers. Basically, what I mean is that at some point people will be so fed up with this neutralization by television and newspapers that the techniques of the 'bush telegraph' will be re-developed, the techniques of transmission by word of mouth. In the framework of this decentred network, this breaking open, what you call a 'post-national' literature will make an impact through diffusion and contamination, not through ideological pressure.

J.D. How does your thesis envisage the relations of domination evolving?

É.G. Creolization includes and goes beyond all possible oppositions. Countries like Switzerland can live in it, countries like Polynesia too. Creolization includes its opposite, uniqueness, which is the principle of all domination. But the actual idea of creolization already fights against this principle. I think that Relation is not virtuous or 'moral' and that a poetics of Relation does not presuppose the immediate and harmonious end of domination. I think that there will always be attempts at domination, but that the way in which they are resisted will change. I think that in the context of globalization the ways of resisting will change. And they will have to be changed because all the ways of resisting that we have known for the past fifty years – and God knows they were heroic, God knows they were sensational – have lapsed into unspeakable horrors, whether in Algeria, in black Africa, in Asia or elsewhere. And we will need to invent new ways of resisting, because it is quite clear that the old ones are no longer any use. I have Algerian friends who exclaim: 'We have had a million deaths for this! We have sacrificed a million lives to end up here!' And God knows it was heroic, that way of liberating oneself, and God knows it was sensational (well, I don't know if God knows, but men know). But it lapsed into the same discord and the same blind relentlessness and the same closed minds as the colonizer offered. We will have to find other ways to resist, without being idealist. The peoples will invent these ways, the Algerians, the Rwandans, the Palestinians, the South Africans, and the others, all the others. I don't want to lapse into idealism. There are concrete resistances that must be undertaken. In the place where one is.

All the rest is Relation: openness and relativity.

Interviews

♦ 5 ♦

The Imagination of Languages*

Lise Gauvin. In *Poétique de la Relation*, you say you were surprised to realize that there are people who are installed in the 'tranquil mass of their language' and who have not experienced that 'torment of *langage*' that you identify in multiple forms. In this context you cite the example of the United States. Don't you think that this torment is more characteristic of people who are called 'peripheral'? Wouldn't it be characteristic of the francophone writers in particular?

Édouard Glissant. It affects the writers who belong to cultural zones in which the language is what I call a composite language. All the languages born of colonization, as for example the Creole languages, are fragile; they are languages which face several problems. First of all, they are subject to contamination from the official language, the language that governs the official life of the community. Then, they are confronted by problems that are apparently very difficult to resolve, problems of stability and transcription. There is a kind of torment of *langage* that accompanies the shift from orality to writing, which weakens us, puts us into a threatening situation where we lose any sense of security, and which means that the people who belong to these cultures are made very sensitive to the problems of *langage*. In the regions where we find old languages, what I call atavistic languages – that is, languages which have developed gradually, which have had the time, through conflicts and agreements, to establish and organize themselves, to find for themselves a form of 'written' classicism – and in the cultures where these languages do not co-exist with composite languages, in the United States for instance, it is very difficult to imagine the torment of languages. Of course, there are countries such as Canada where two of

---

* This interview took place in Pointe-à-Pitre in December 1991. It has already appeared in the issue of the journal Études françaises entitled 'L'Amérique entre les langues' (vol. 28, no. 2/3, 1992–1993).

these languages confront each other and where one dominates the other, for example the English language in relation to the French language in Quebec. In this case, a speaker of the dominated language will be more sensitive to the problematic of languages. Whenever one explicitly links the problem of language to the problem of identity one makes a mistake, in my opinion, because precisely what characterizes our times is what I call the imagination of languages, in other words, the awareness of all the world's languages. I think that in eighteenth- and nineteenth-century Europe, even when a French writer knew English or Italian or German, he did not taken these languages into account in his writing. Writing was monolingual. Today, even when a writer does not know any other language, he takes account, whether he realizes it or not, of the existence of these languages around him in his writing process. One can no longer write a language monolingually. One is obliged to take into account the imaginations of the languages. These imaginations strike us through all kinds of new, unprecedented ways: audiovisual media, radio, television. When one sees an African landscape, even if one does not know the Bantu language, for instance, there is something of that language which, through the landscape we are seeing, strikes us and calls to us, even if we have never heard a single word of Bantu. And when we see the landscapes of the Australian plateau, even if we do not know a single word of the language of the Australian aboriginals, we are impregnated with something that comes from there. One can no longer write one's landscape or describe one's own language monolingually. People like the Americans of the United States, who do not imagine the problematic of languages, do not even imagine the world. Some of the defenders of Creole are completely closed to this problematic. They want to defend Creole in a monolingual way, the same way as those who have linguistically oppressed them. They inherit this sectarian monolingualism and they defend their language, in my view, in the wrong way. My position on the question is that we will not save one language in a country by letting the others perish. My position is that there is solidarity between all the threatened languages, including the Anglo-American language, which is just as much affected as French is by the hegemony of the international convention of Anglo-American. I believe that solidarity exists between all the world's languages, and that what is beautiful about the chaos-world, what I call the chaos-world today, is this meeting, these bursts of light, these explosions, whose economy or principles we have not yet managed to grasp. Some people are sensitive to the problematic of languages because they are sensitive to the problematic of the chaos-world. Some people are not sensitive to it, either because they are enclosed in the communicative power of their own language – this is the case of people in the United States – or because they promote their language in a monolingual and angry way: this is the case of some of the defenders of Creole, and also of some of the defenders of the French language in Quebec, forced into this by the situation. They are blind to the real situation in the world, in what I call the chaos-world, this conflictual and wonderful meeting of languages, blind to all these bursts of light that spring from it, and of which, I repeat, we have not yet begun to really grasp the imagination nor even to understand the principles.

L.G. Is the French writer, or are or certain French writers from France also aware of this problematic?

É.G. I don't think so. At least, I don't know of many examples. This problematic of the imagination of languages does of course have a tradition in the West. It goes back quite a long way. I think Beckett would be an example of this. Artaud is another one: he did a lot to deconstruct the language. Also Ezra Pound, in the United States. The last texts of Joyce, like *Anna Livia Plurabelle*, are purely and simply thickets of language in which we must wander and carve out a path for ourselves. So, it is perceptible in the evolution of Western sensibility, but I think that at the present time in Europe it has been lost, because the real has encountered the imaginary project as this was set up by Joyce or Beckett. The other languages are there. But what dominates today in the European and French panorama is not this imagination but a rather flat kind of folkloric reality: the French public is totally impressed and fascinated by para-exotic creations that are very common and even slightly vulgar. The more a writer fills his text with extremely facile quasi-exotic references to the existence of his language, which is usually, let's say, an oppressed mother tongue, the happier the public will be. Which often provokes a certain irritation: it's chasing after shadows, it's very superficial, it gets rid of the problem without having to solve it. But sometimes, what else is there to do? Perhaps future precepts will spring from these excessive accumulations.

L.G. Where does folklorization begin? Where does exoticism begin? Does this mean that there is a good and a bad use of exoticism?

É.G. Certainly. If we move a little out of the linguistic domain, we know since Segalen and other authors that exoticism can be completely negative or completely inspiring. I often read books that don't irritate me but do leave me cold, because one feels very clearly that they are fabrications around these conflicts of *langage*, and that this kind of drama of the situation of languages in their relation to one another only intervenes very occasionally. As always, folklorization is the surface covering of what is churning away in the depths. A pretence.

L.G. A moment ago you used the expression 'thicket', thicket of languages. Can you say which languages you have had to go through to get to the point where you could write?

É.G. First of all I had to go through the echo, the memory of the Creole language as I heard it in my childhood from the Creole story-tellers. I say the memory because, although I continued to use this language in my childhood and adolescence, the way Creole was deployed in the folk tale was not the same as in ordinary life. And when I study, for instance, the phenomena of colonization in Antillean discourse, I refer (as a site of resistance) more to the *langage* of the storyteller than to everyday *langage*. Also, in the Creole folk tales that I heard in my childhood, there were cabbalistic phrases that had probably been inherited from African languages, whose meaning no-one understood, and which had a powerful effect on the audience without anyone knowing why. It is quite obvious to me, now, that I was influenced by this unexplained presence of languages or phrases whose meaning you do not know and which nevertheless have a strong effect on you, and it is perhaps possible that a large part of my theories on the necessary opacities of *langage* stem from there. I also had to go through, at school, the influence of Rimbaud's and Mallarmé's poetics, and I had to carry out a process of reflection on myself in relation to these poetics. And then, I had to go through the presence of Faulkner's work, an English-language work that I have deeply immersed myself in, like many other modern contemporary writers, and this is interesting because I find I can immediately gain access to the structure of Faulkner's work before gaining access to its literal meanings. I believe that the translations of Faulkner, the admirable French translations, no doubt lose something of the *langage*, the *langage* of the Mississippi and its distinctive features, but that they nonetheless have the merit of bringing out very clearly the work's structure. One can gain access to the structure of a work without really knowing its *langage*, and it is this that means we can say that we can no longer write in a monolingual fashion. We write in the presence of a number of structures of works, such as Faulkner's, even if we don't have a good knowledge of the language in which this work is embodied, even if we are not capable of appreciating the distinctive features of the *langage* that the work uses. I have had to carve my way through all these dense thickets before building my own *langage*.

L.G. In your novel *Malemort* we read: 'We cannot name anything, we have without realizing it been worn out in ourselves, our way of speaking is impossible and sought after'. Isn't there from the start a kind of consciousness of lack, despite the words of the story-tellers?

É.G. But at that point I am talking about the conventional *langage* of the educated and those who speak for the community. It's true that traditionally we were, we Antilleans, in a blocked language, a language frozen into a respectful attitude towards the French norm, and that in our mouths this language was perfect, grammatically perfect. It was totally correct, and yet the use of the language was completely false and disfigured. It wasn't a living language, it was like a dead language. And then there was also the fact that the elites, the old elites that spoke these languages, never took any account of all the realities of our lives. We had never reflected on the real presence of our landscapes, from the point of view of our imagination, our sensibility. We had never reflected on the density of our own histories. We more or less followed the track of History with a capital H, as defined by the West. There were all these kinds of lack that we had to struggle against and I think I can say that I, along with others, have tried to make up for these lacks, to reconstruct something different.

L.G. All the same, is there not a tradition of earlier Antillean writing to which you belong?

É.G. There isn't a tradition that I belong to, but I do think that there is a continuum of discontinuity, if I can use such a byzantine formula, which has meant that our literature has not simply accumulated. We have had nothing but jolts, spurts, and kind of spikes, vertical falls into the abyss. For example, there was initially a break between the speech of the Creole storyteller and the first written texts. We had to overcome this hiatus, to come back to the subject matter of the folk tale. We do not have a literary continuum. That's what makes me say that we can enter easily into modernity, that we are not atavistic. In French literature, one can say that the language has an atavistic fluidity, that the language of Madame de Sévigny or the language of Colette has the same way of writing French, so luminous and totally at ease with itself. We don't have that, and this fact determines new conditions of literary practice, in which everything that is chaotic, everything that we call baroque, comes naturally to us. We do not choose, through a kind of will, to go against atavistic fluidity. There is a kind of baroque, in Artaud for instance, that is a reaction against that fluidity; with us, it is not a reaction, it is a natural manner of being and expressing ourselves. We do not derive our continuity from constructed works, but paradoxically from the historical impossibility of continuity.

L.G. And these jolts and spurts have not taken a particular form, don't have any particular name?

É.G. I don't think so. There are the Creole folk tales, there are certain chroniclers who are important even *a contrario*, but I don't really think so … Basically, contemporary Antillean literature begins in the period immediately after the war, with writers like Césaire and Damas. But there were also the works of the novelists of rural society, like Tardon or Zobel. They seem to me important only because of their exhaustive inventory of the real, which has meant that we have not had to start again with this inventory of the real in the manner of French realism. Their works are very important in so far as they have freed us from the concern that we should go on depicting reality. If writers like Césaire or Damas never did that, it's because it had already been done before them. Today, from the Creole storyteller to Tardon, to Césaire, to the writers who are just beginning to write, we reconstitute the continuity, and we see it as open to other places.

L.G. In Éloge de la créolité we find the expression 'writing towards the difficult'. Does this difficulty affect your own activity as a writer?

É.G. Yes, because we are not practitioners of writing, we are practitioners of orality. One always forgets this banal, well-known fact, which is so obvious. The Antillean storyteller is called a master of the spoken word, literally. But we had forgotten this, and when we had to switch to writing ['passer à l'écriture'], as one talks about acting out ['passer à l'acte'] in psychoanalysis, we were confronted with this absence of signposts, of traditions, of a continuum of writing. If a contemporary French writer reacts against Malherbe, Voltaire, Chateaubriand or Victor Hugo, and if he wants to go back, as a reference or a counter-reference, to Rabelais or the rhetoricians of the Middle Ages, he can do so without difficulty because he has behind him this continuum, this tradition and this counter-tradition that are written into his history and the history of his sensibility. But as for us, we only had the crude problem to overcome, the absolutely 'abnormal' problem of an orality that had not yet found its rules of writing. That is and always has been our problem. Western literatures dealt with this transition a long time ago. French literature lived through the drama, in the noble sense of the term, of the transition from oral to written in the time of Rutebeuf, Villon and the Pléiade poets. It was then that they had to create in an exaggerated sense: all the peculiarities of the Pléiade come from this, these sorts of monstrosities, fabrications of words ... We had to start again from the beginning of all that. We have to constitute very quickly something that took seven centuries to be formed in the case of French language and literature.

L.G. That explains a sort of distrust in your writing of stylistic excesses and also of what you call verbal amplitude. There is a kind of desire to stay as close as possible.

É.G. Because the rhetoric of the French language was imposed on us and because we were taught the French language in a perfect, exaggerated, frozen manner. And this rhetoric of the French language whose idea was imposed on us is an extra negative element; we had to react against it. Using this rhetoric imposed on us the idea that French was the only language that could express something of our realities. We had to fight against that to discover that the poetics of Creole, of the Creole languages, could express something just as well and that a new poetics could emerge that would be a combination, a synthesis of Creole and French poetics, in other words the poetics, rhetorics and counter-rhetorics that are internal to the French language. This is why we are sensitive to the problematic of languages, we, the francophone Antillean writers. It is not the same for the anglophone Antillean writers. First of all because for these anglophone writers, Creole is a fairly distant presence, except for writers like Derek Walcott in St Lucia, an anglophone country but where they speak the same Creole as in Martinique, more or less. But St Lucian Creole is not related to the English language, which gives the poet a greater 'ease'. And the Jamaican, Trinidadian, etc., writers are less aware of this problematic of languages because in these regions the Creole language disappeared fairly early on and so for a long time they have spoken only English.* We have seen how their 'Creole' perverts the norms of the English language from the inside, reforming it. The creolization that they experience is one that by-passes language: it is cultural, social, involving customs and behaviour, but it is not linguistic creolization. But we come together at the end of our paths: in the rise of a new *langage*, to be shared.

L.G. What does 'subverting the language' mean to you?

É.G. The subversion comes from creolization (here, linguistic) and not from creolisms. What people tend to take from creolization is the creolism, that is: introducing Creole words into the French language, inventing new French words on the basis of Creole words. I feel that this is the exotic aspect of the question. And I would also make this criticism of some Quebecker writers. Creolization for me is not the creolism; it is, for example, generating a *langage* that weaves together the poetics, maybe the conflicting poetics, of the Creole and French languages. What do I call a poetics? The Creole storyteller uses techniques that are alien to the spirit of the French language, are even the opposite of it: techniques of repetition, intensification, going over and over the same things, keeping the reader in suspense, circularity. The practice of listing that Saint-John Perse uses in his poetics and that I outline in many of my texts, these lists that try to exhaustively capture the real not in a formula but in an accumulation, accumulation as a rhetorical technique, precisely – all this seems to me far more important from the point of view of the definition of a new *langage*, but far less visible. So that the French reader faced with such texts may say to himself: 'I can't understand anything', and indeed he does not understand anything because these poetics are not something he can perceive whereas he can perceive a creolism straight away. He can find it amusing, he can say: 'Oh yes, that's interesting'. He has taken a word, he has taken it apart, and that can even seem exotic to him. But the poetics, the structure of the *langage*, the reworking of the structure of the *langages*, will seem to him purely and simply obscure. The accumulation of parentheses, for instance, or interpolations, which is a technique, does not intervene so decisively in

---

* In fact Jamaican and Trinidadian Creoles are still widely spoken today and conform to Glissant's definition of Creole as 'a language whose constitutive elements are mutually heterogeneous' (see also p. 9).

French discourse. When I am asked: 'Who do you write for?', it makes me laugh because I don't write for this or that kind of reader, I try to write with a view to that moment when the reader or the listener – more and more texts will no doubt be recorded – becomes open to all kinds of poetics and not only the poetics of his own language. And that day will come when there will be a kind of infinite variation of linguistic sensibilities. Not a knowledge of languages, that's something else. More and more, translation will become an essential art. Up to now we have left translation too much just to the translators, we must get poets involved in it as well. Translations will become an important part of poetics, which is not the case today. And I think of all the infinite variation of nuances of the possible poetics of languages, and everyone will be more and more imbued with it, not only with the poetics and the economy, the structure and economy of one's own language, but by all this fragrance, all this explosion of the poetics of the world. It will be a new sensibility. I believe that the writer today is trying to foresee this, to prepare for it and to accustom himself to it.

L.G. Basically what is important to emphasize is that when you say 'the words of relation are multilingual', this multilingualism is not a juxtaposition of languages.

É.G. Whenever I talk about multilingualism, someone immediately asks me: 'Ah! yes, how many languages do you speak?' It's not a question of speaking the languages, that's not the problem. It may be that one speaks no language except one's own. It is rather the actual way in which one speaks one's own language, speaking it in a closed or open way; speaking it in ignorance of the presence of other languages or in the prescient awareness that the other languages exist and that they influence us even without our realizing it. It is not a question of science, of the knowledge of languages, it is a question of the imagination of languages. It is not a question of the juxtaposition of languages, but of connecting them with each other.

L.G. Isn't it the same kind of misunderstanding that makes the use of creolisms and the vernacular very easily recuperated, and often associated with regionalisms and slang?

É.G. It's a pity because that removes the central problem, the fundamental problem, which is the problem of poetics. Creolisms, particularisms, regionalisms are all ways of satisfying, on the scale of the hierarchy of languages, the great languages of culture. And people are very satisfied. Because this way, the essential problem is not addressed – the problem of poetics, that is, the non-hierarchical use of different poetics in different languages. Nobody wants to talk about this because it renders null and void the pretentious belief in the superiority of some languages over others. Creolisms and regionalisms cannot open this debate; on the contrary, they consecrate the pre-eminence of some languages over others. So that there would be languages of noble usage, and languages which can produce only regionalisms, particularisms. Well, it's not true. In the modern context, all languages are regional and all languages have their poetics, at the same time.

L.G. Do you see a difference between prose and poetry, in the treatment of the language?

É.G. In the exercise of prose, as far as our literatures are concerned, writers are too ready to believe that description of the real renders account of the real. It's a bit like painters who portray a way of life, or genre paintings: a tropical market or Antillean fishermen. They think that by doing this they are rendering account of reality. It's not at all true. They absolutely do not render account of reality; reality is something different from this appearance. In fact, poetry is up to now the only art that can really go behind appearances. I believe that this is one of its vocations. It's the determination to dismantle genres, this categorization that has been so profitable, so fruitful in the case of Western literatures. I believe that we can write poems that are essays, essays that are novels, novels that are poems. I mean that we try to dismantle genres precisely because we can feel that the roles that have been allocated to these genres in Western literature are no longer helpful for our investigation, which is not only an investigation of the real, but is also an investigation of imagination, of the depths, the unsaid, the taboos. We must 'bump along' ['cahoter'] in the sense of a bumpy road, but also of chaos ['chaos'], of what is chaotic. We must bump along all these genres in order to express what we want to express. And in that sense, we necessarily leave behind us the conventions of prose, but also the conventions of poetry. Poetry can be bumpy/chaotic ['chaoteuse']; prose can be dreamy and fall into a kind of torment, of swirling, of intoxication, while still remaining meaningful. I think that we will invent new genres of which we as yet have no idea.

L.G. Éloge de la créolité is a manifesto which quotes you a lot, which uses your work, but don't you also say that, on some points, you do not agree with the signatories?

É.G. The arguments to be found in the Éloge de la créolité are certainly inspired by *Le Discours antillais* or by *L'Intention poétique*, or even *Soleil de la conscience*, in other words my essays, and the signatories of the manifesto have thus certainly acknowledged that they are indebted to them. But I think there has been a misunderstanding because in *Le Discours antillais* I talked a lot about creolization. For me, *créolité* is a different interpretation of creolization. Creolization is a perpetual movement of cultural and linguistic interpenetrability, which means that one never ends up with a definition of Being. My criticism of Negritude was that it defined Being: the Negro Being ... I believe that there is no more 'Being'. The Being is a great, noble, boundless invention of the West, and in particular of Greek philosophy. The definition of Being was soon to give rise, in Western history, to all sorts of sectarianisms, metaphysical absolutes and fundamentalisms whose catastrophic effects we can see today. I think we have to say that there is no longer anything but the being, that is, particular existences that correspond, that enter into conflict, and that we must abandon the claim that we can define Being. But, that is what *créolité* does: it defines a Creole Being. It is a kind of regression, from the point of view of the process, but one that is perhaps necessary in order to defend the position of Creoles today. Just as Negritude had a vital importance for the defence of African values and those of the black diaspora. In similar fashion, I have not wanted to agree to the definition of a Negro Being while there are Negro beings that cannot necessarily all be put in the same category: an Antillean is not a Senegalese, a black Brazilian is not a black American. I am stating the obvious, but it is to illustrate my proposition that we must give up the absolutist claim, often sectarian, to be able to define Being. The world is creolizing, all cultures are creolizing at the present time in their contacts with one another. The ingredients vary, but the basic principle is that today there is no longer a single culture that can claim to be pure.

L.G. What do you think of the notion of transculture?

É.G. The notion of transculture is not adequate. Basically, the term creolization covers this notion of transculture. But the notion of transculture suggests that one could calculate and predict the results of a transculturalization; whereas creolization in my view is unpredictable. It always produces something more, which means that what is produced is unpredictable in relation to the component elements. I distinguish creolization from two other domains: on the one hand, transculture in the strict sense, and on the other, hybridity in the physiological or racial domain. One can predict, or try to predict, the results of hybridization. One does so in science when one attempts a synthesis: when one crossbreeds a red bean with a green bean, one can calculate the results. Creolization is unpredictable: one cannot calculate the results. That is the difference, in my view, between creolization and, on the one hand, hybridity, and on the other, transculture. One can access transculturation vie the concept, but one can only access creolization through the imagination. And I believe that the concept, in our present time, has to be fertilized by the imagination.

L.G. Hence the role of the writer ...

É.G. And hence the role of the poet who seeks out not predictable results but imaginations open to all sorts of futures of creolization. The poet is not afraid of unpredictability.

L.G. One last question: how do you view the fate of languages in the future?

É.G. One cannot set oneself up as a prophet. I think that the fate of languages is linked to the relation between orality and writing. Perhaps the book will disappear as a concrete form of knowledge in our societies. It is quite possible that the book will die and that in thirty years' time readers (of books) will organize themselves as sects in catacombs, disapproved of by public morality. It is possible that, from this point of view, books are already almost clandestine receptacles of the organicity of languages, and that the public side of languages, their audiovisual impact, is already that of codes, rather like the highway code, the gastronomic code, etc. Languages are becoming impoverished. My hope is that this kind of fragmentation, of variations, the infinite multiplicity of contacts and conflicts between languages, will give birth to a new imagination of human speech which will perhaps transcend languages. I don't want to be a prophet, but I think that one day human sensibility will move towards *langages* that will overtake languages, that will integrate all sorts of dimensions, forms, silences, representations, and will become so many new elements of language.

♦ 6 ♦

The Writer and the Breath of Place*

Lise Gauvin. How would you classify this book, *Tout-monde*? Is it a novel, a fresco? How would you describe it?

Édouard Glissant. The publishers call it a novel; so I suppose the public can consider it as that. There are series of stories narrated in the book and intercut with each other, series of itineraries, series of trajectories, a kind of wandering by the characters, but which all start from Martinique and finish in Martinique. I think it really is a novel, but a novel that has burst apart. You know, we've all had enough of the old route of novels that begin in one place, then follow set movements and end up in a sort of rhetorical pre-ordained destiny. What is exciting about the novel today is that it can go off in all directions: it travels all over the world. I don't see how a novel whose title is *Tout-monde* [Whole-World] could be linear and conventional as novels were at the start of this century. No, it's a novel that engages with the substance of the world, that is as expansive as the substance of the world, and I don't have a problem with that. It is also a work that risks going beyond established literary genres. Who knows?

L.G. You talk about wandering. Could you define for us these words that recur often in your books, namely: drift, 'drive', wandering?

É.G. Wandering and drift are, let's say, the appetite for the world. What makes us trace out paths just about everywhere in the world. Drift is also the being's openness towards all sorts of possible migrations. 'Drive', as experienced and conceived of in Martinique itself, is a word derived from

---

* This interview took place at Le Diamant (Martinique) in December 1993, shortly after the publication of *Tout-monde*. Part of it was broadcast on Radio-Canada on 22 March 1995.

'drift' ['dérive'], and which has become a Creole word. 'Drive' is openness, fragility, the determination to keep moving and the reluctance to declare, to decide in an imperial fashion. And wandering is what inclines the being to abandon systematic thought for a way of thinking – not exploratory, because that has a colonialist connotation – but that investigates the real: thinking as travelling, which is also a thinking based on ambiguity and uncertainty which saves us from systematic thought with its intolerance and sectarianism. Wandering has virtues that I would call the virtues of totality – the will, the desire, the passion to know the totality, to know the 'Whole-World' – but also virtues of self-preservation in the sense that we do not intend to know the 'Whole-World' in order to dominate it, to give it a single meaning. Thinking as wandering saves us from systematic thought.

L.G. So the 'Whole-World' would be this desire to know, to get closer to the totality of the world?

É.G. It is the totality of the world as it exists in its reality and as it exists in our desire.

L.G. And who desires in this book? There is a whole range of figurations of the writer. You talk about the poet, the delirious speaker ['déparleur'], the inventor and the chronicler. There are also some texts signed Mathieu Béluse. Who is speaking in this novel? Isn't there a sort of chain of speakers or talkers?

É.G. The book is constructed in such a way that one cannot tell who is speaking. At first it was said that the author is speaking. Then that 'Someone is speaking'. Then even that 'it is speaking', in the psycho-analytical sense of the id. And there was always this individuation or this neutralization of the person speaking. I think the problem is that the person speaking is multiple. There is not someone who speaks, it is not the author speaking, it is not the id speaking. What or who speaks is multiple; one cannot know where he is coming from; even he himself may not know, and he does not control or direct the production of his speech. What is projected as speech meets up with another multiplicity which is the multiplicity of the world. When one designs a poetics of diversity as I am claiming to do, one cannot speak from the point of view of uniqueness.

That is why there is this multiplicity of speakers. The paradox is that all of this starts from one place and comes back to it, moving in a circle.

L.G. Could this concept of diversity, this concept of the 'Whole-World' and the totality of the world, lead to the abolition of the idea of the nation? What happens to the idea of the nation in this context?

É.G. It could not lead to the abolition of identities because the 'Whole-World', diversity, is not a magma or a confusion in which everything gets lost. If one enters the diversity of the world having renounced one's own identity, one gets lost in a sort of confusion. Identities are one of the victories of modern times, a painful victory because it is not finished and because all over the face of the planet there are nodes, pockets of desolation that work against this movement. But there is also a movement that I would describe like this: single root identities are gradually giving way to relation-identities, that is to say, rhizome-identities. It's not a matter of uprooting oneself, but of conceiving the root as less intolerant, less sectarian: a root-identity that does not kill everything around it but on the contrary extends its branches towards others. What, following Deleuze and Guattari, I call a rhizome-identity. In this context, it is certainly true that the idea of the nation acquires a content that is far more cultural than to do with the state, military, economic or political, far less patriotic in the traditional sense of the term. This is why today we can talk about a Basque nation even though up until now there has never been a Basque state. One can exist as an identity without existing as a power. The idea of power linked to identity is beginning to erode, to disappear. People will say that this is utopia and that, in any case, if one has no power there is no point in having an identity; I don't think that is true. And I think we are seeing more and more that great powers can disappear as such while the nations, in the cultural sense of the word, continue to exist. But this single root-identity, which has done us so much harm, is still raging and laying waste to the earth, as in Yugoslavia.

L.G. Identity does not necessarily lead on to the idea of a country but there are also identities that disappear. In what situation, in what conditions, does identity persist without disappearing?

É.G. We are in a time – I call it world-time – in which we can no longer impose conditions on the world. That doesn't mean that we no longer have a framework in which to act, or limits to an action, but one can no longer project on to the world those large-scale ideological schemas that would have formed the basis for our work. I believe that is impossible. It is one of the common places of world-thought. It seems to me that until the world-totality is realized, that is, until all the world's cultures have understood that it is not necessary to annihilate, to eradicate another's culture in order to assert oneself, cultures will be in danger. Until one accepts the idea, not only as a concept but in the imagination of human communities, that the world-totality is a rhizome in which everyone needs everyone else, it is obvious that there will be cultures which are in danger. What I am saying is that it is neither through force nor through concepts that one will protect these cultures, but through the imagination of the world-totality, that is to say, through the lived necessity of this fact: that all cultures need all other cultures.

L.G. So there is a particular role given to the writer: to think the imagination of the world?

É.G. Not to think it but to express it. In order to express it, he has to think it, but it's not an informative thought, it's a thought that can be intuitive, that can take on very particular forms, forms that stem from a place. We don't live in the air, we don't live in the clouds around the earth, we live in places. One has to start from a place and imagine the world-totality. This place, which is crucial, must not be a territory from which one looks at one's neighbour across a totally closed frontier and with the subconscious desire to go to the other in order to bring him to one's own ideas or impulses. I think this is a change in the imagination of human communities that we must all achieve. Now people will say to me: 'This is utopian; there are political, military and economic powers and this whole machine will go on crushing, grinding up the world-totality to make it into a kind of uniform flour.' OK, that's true, it's true, but I am saying that we cannot fight that machine with the same means (of sectarian uniqueness), but only by changing the imagination, the mentality and the impulses of human communities today.

L.G. Isn't it imagination that brings us to this poetics of chaos that you talk about? Chaos in itself is neither beautiful nor ugly, but when you say:

'Chaos is beautiful', are you not referring to a sort of organization of the totality by the imagination?

É.G. Chaos is beautiful on condition that one tries through imagination to track down, to trace out, not its laws but its invariants. Rather like the way in which the physicists and the experts in chaos theory try to conceive of the physical universe. There are invariants and these invariants are beautiful. You can try to track them down starting from your own place, your own land which is not a territory, your own imagination which is particular to you and touches everyone else's imagination. That is what makes it beautiful. It's beautiful because there are invariants that one can try to find. It's a great challenge.

L.G. What would be an example of an invariant?

É.G. The fact that just about everywhere on the surface of the earth, in all countries, people are abandoning the land in favour of huge cities. That is an invariant. Both beautiful and terrifying. There are absolutely no exceptions and perhaps one day there will be a return, a movement in the opposite direction, a re-appropriation of the land, not as territory but as land (what one calls the countryside) with a view to reformulating somewhat, restructuring the human imagination. That is an invariant, a negative one, but it is an invariant. It is happening in all the cultures of the world, whether they are developed or under-developed, isolated or in contact. There are positive invariants as well. In all the cultures of the world today, people are worried – in an obsessional way, or a neurotic way, or a very intellectual way, or a natural way, without really thinking about it – by a sort of need to clean things up, which the ecologists are echoing in an organized fashion: a need to return to more obvious, simpler things. Which can take on reactionary aspects, identitarian aspects closed in on themselves, it's true. There are invariants whose existence we do not yet suspect. It is perhaps the role of poetics to point to these, to search for them. It is the function of the common places of world-thought to illuminate this research. In doing this work, what are we giving up? We are giving up the claim to find truth solely within the narrow circle of our own subjectivity, and I think that this too is an invariant, this necessity to go beyond one's own subjectivity, not towards a totalitarian system but towards the intersubjectivity of the 'Whole-World'. The role of all literature is to join in this search.

L.G. By means of poetics?

É.G. By poetics. We will see that poetics is not an art of dreams and illusions, but that it is a way of thinking about oneself, conceiving one's relation to oneself and to the other, and expressing it. Every poetics is a network.

L.G. I recently heard you say: 'There will be no more classicism'. What does that mean exactly? How do you see literatures evolving?

É.G. It means that all literatures, especially in the Western and European world, have implicitly been supported by the idea that the values expressed by a literature particular to a given culture, or a national literature where there are nations, that the values of every literature are underpinned by the secret hope that its values will become universal values, valid for everyone. It seems to me that this is the wrong way to use place. Place is crucial but it is not exportable, from the point of view of values. One can't generalize from particular values but one can quantify all these kinds of particular values, not in order to 'extract' universal values from them but to make them into a rhizome, a field, a cloth, a weave of values that are different but are constantly touching and intertwining with each other. That's not the same as thinking that one's own value will become a universal value. Thinking that one's own value enters into an intertwining of the values of the totality of the world is in my view a much greater, more noble and generous project than that of trying to make one's own value become valid for the whole world. Classicism, for me, is what happens when a particular value wants and tries to be a universally valid value. I believe we must abandon the idea of the universal. The universal is an illusion, a deceptive dream. We must conceive of the world-totality as a totality, that is, as a realized quantity and not a value abstracted from particular values. This is fundamental and, without our realizing it, it changes most of the facts concerning world literature in our times.

L.G. At the same time as resisting the notion of the universal, don't you equally resist the notion of regionalism within which people try to enclose the francophone writers, in particular? They are often classified as regional, regionalist, peripheral, etc. writers.

É.G. That is a completely obsolete discourse. I believe that the continents are turning into archipelagos beyond national frontiers. There are some regions which detach themselves and which culturally take on more importance than the nations enclosed within their frontiers. For instance, in Europe, it is perfectly obvious that national frontiers are tending to fade away but that the regions are beginning to appear. These regions are still suffering from the existence of the nations, which tend to make them peripheral, precisely, to consider them as dependent on a centre. I think that, for example, some of the most striking thoughts recently have been formulated from what I have called peripheries in relation to centres. These centres are less and less productive themselves, less and less important or present in our thinking. Regional thought becomes central thought, so that in fact there is no longer any centre or periphery. One can no longer write *Itinéraire de Paris à Jérusalem*.* One can even imagine the opposite. But to imagine the opposite would also be to fall back into the old schema. In the rhizome of the world-totality, centre and peripheries are obsolete notions. The old reflexes are still active but these old reflexes seem more and more ridiculous and ineffectual. That is my first observation. The existence of regions that are turning continents into archipelagos means that continental thought is less and less dense, thick and weighty, while archipelagic thought is more and more effervescent and proliferating. There is this system which is disintegrating and rebuilding itself as a non-systematic reality on the one hand, but on the other, there is the fact that this regionalization, in the good sense, is still linked to the old idea of the single root-identity, and that some of the regions that have recently reasserted themselves tend to set themselves up as nations which are just as sectarian and intolerant as the old nations. There are sudden advances and no less sudden retreats but I think we are proceeding – let's not say proceeding, that's still a systematic thought, an ideological thought – let's say we are orientating ourselves, in the sense of the 'Orient', orientating ourselves towards situations where regional cultural realities will no longer be considered either as peripheries or as centres, but as effervescent – there is no other word – multiplicities of the reality of the world-totality.

L.G. Would you agree that for writers, let's say, of the periphery, there is in spite of everything the threat of folklorization, either from the inside or

---

* A travel book published by François-René de Chateaubriand in 1811.

more or less imposed from the outside by readers' or the public's expectations? How do you view this problem of folklorization?

É.G. Folklorization is the result of the fact that the transition from dispossession to personal autonomy is realized in two ways: on the one hand as though driven by the necessity of transformation into a nation, a force, a power, and this restricts the 'Being' to concise, basic formulations, which he believes hold the secret of a real transformation whereas he is in fact doing nothing except following the old models; and, on the other hand, by the belief that one cannot achieve anything unless one has the approval and the attention of the old centres. For that reason they do everything they can, whether in the domain of *langage* or the domain of putting forward ideas, to ensure that the old centre is both slightly taken aback and convinced by what they say, even if what they say, what they express, does not necessarily go in the direction of the poetics of the world-totality. As a result they often create other forms of regionalism which should be banished. True regionalization must not depend on a centre or set itself up as a centre. It must be a poetics of sharing in the Whole-World. This is quite difficult for the communities to see and quite difficult to put into practice given the economic and political demands of collective existence.

L.G. Isn't there a paradox, precisely: the periphery wanting to be what it is without being dependent on any external recognition, while the writer, especially the Antillean writer for example, still depends on Europe to gain recognition, to get his work known more widely? The 'Carrefour des littératures européennes' is in Strasbourg, and at the moment everything still goes through the channel of French distribution.

É.G. The Carrefour des littératures européennes took place in Strasbourg but the International Writers' Parliament which was created there won't just stay in Strasbourg. It will be a travelling international parliament. That means that even if it started in Strasbourg, with a very small selection of the world's writers, in its travels the parliament will have to bring together a large number of the world's writers, otherwise it will disappear, obviously. It's a creation which corresponds to the facts of the world at present, but it is not certain that this parliament will last. If it cannot rally a large part of the world-totality, the parliament will fade away. Nor can we, from the point of view of logistics and the production of ideas, behave as though these old centres didn't exist. Strasbourg, a European focus point, is important for everyone. The old centres have their traditional strength and it would be pure folklore to shut oneself away in an isolation that refused to recognize their necessary participation. The only thing is, we must no longer think of them as centres: we must think of them as participating elements. It's also true that writers are still dependent on these centres, because that is where the publishing houses are, and the distribution circuits, the poles of the reverberation and illustration of the works. But we no longer confer on them any legitimacy as poles, and that is what is important. One can have centres with the power of reverberation, but if these centres no longer have the legitimacy of the reverberation, as I believe is the case, then we can work with them and see what we can do. In any case, these centres, these poles of reverberation need the voices that come from elsewhere and they operate more and more through those voices. Latin-American, Japanese, Caribbean, North American etc. literatures are more and more actively involved in the reverberation of the world-totality, and participate just as strongly as voices coming from Europe or anywhere else.

L.G. Can't that have an influence on poetics? One notices that in your latest book, as in the preceding ones, there are no footnotes, no italics, no explanatory glossary, things that one does see with other writers. There are not really any creolisms in your writing. How do you react to this type of literature?

É.G. I think we are all probably going towards the Whole-World but there are different speeds, different moments. If we all went towards the Whole-World at the same rate, that would be regimentation and the Whole-World would be boringly and annoyingly uniform. In my opinion, it's all going in the same direction, as regards the literary work. Literatures that are just beginning, with surprising specificity and glossaries at the end of the book, will evolve towards a time when the *langage* will be less ostentatious, when they won't feel the need to have footnotes or endnotes, and when the reality of the world will be there as in other books, without explanations. But that cannot come about in one single movement, all at once. Otherwise there would be an absolutely exhausting monotony. We need to have these upheavals, these advances, these retreats, these clashes, these harmonies that are all interesting to trace out in the development of the world's literatures.

L.G. Would you say that your own writing is fed by the breath of Creole and of French, that it is the same breath, one could almost say merged into one?

É.G. There comes a time when the breath of the place – let's call it that, since I've told you that for me place is after all crucial – the breath of the place meets other breaths and is transformed in that meeting. In my own case, for example, I have paid great attention to two voices that belong to writers who represent the complete opposite of what I am trying to do. They are Saint-John Perse and William Faulkner. They are two Plantation writers, in Martinique we would say two 'békés', two planter or settler writers who at first sight occupy a place that is completely closed to me. And yet, these two writers seem to me decisively important in all the work that I am trying to collect together. I have explained this often. Sooner or later the breath that you breathe, that serves to express you, transforms itself. If it does not transform itself it is not a breath, it is a stagnant smell and stagnant smells produce neither poetics nor literature. As for my way of envisaging the poetics of Creole and of French, it aims not to stagnate; I am always concerned to move on towards the 'Whole-World'. I think that this is what distinguishes defences of regionalization in the direction of the 'Whole-World', which are very beautiful, from defences of regionalisms that only relate to oneself and end up as new forms of intolerance, new forms of stagnation.

L.G. Could you remind us of the distinction you make between multilingualism and polyglossia?

É.G. What I want to express when I say that we write in the presence of all the world's languages is that there is a new criterion affecting the existence and the function of the writer: it's not that we know all the languages or a large number of them, it's that we become aware in the world-totality that languages are disappearing, and that with them it's a part of the human imagination that disappears. Our way of defending languages must be multilingual. We must defend our languages in the name of multilingualisms and not in the name of an intolerant monolingualism. That for me is the decisive dimension: because one will not save any one language of the world by letting the others perish. What has to be changed is the imagination of human communities, so that they accept the fact that we need all the languages. If we don't do this work, we will all be swallowed up by the devouring wave of an international pidgin that may be Anglo-American, or may be something else, but which will in any case absorb all other languages. I always say that the first victim of Anglo-American pidgin is the English language; that we must consider multilingualism as a poetic reality of our existence and not as the fact that we are polyglots, that we speak several languages. In fact the poetics of languages is perhaps not very apparent to an interpreter who knows seven or eight languages; there is perhaps more poetics in the nostalgia of not knowing a language than in the actual practice of the language. That is the difference between multilingualism and polyglossia. In Strasbourg, there were polyglots who spoke four, five, six languages, but everyone was aware or sensed that we need all the languages and that every time a language disappears, even if we have never heard it spoken, even if we do not speak it, we are impoverished by that disappearance.

L.G. On a quite different subject, what does it mean to you to have such an enormous legacy, to see that writers claim to follow you?

É.G. That's just the effects of publicity, I'm not sure that it corresponds to reality.

L.G. But surely, you have in a way created a school …

É.G. What does that mean, to create a school? It means that there are people who 'follow' you along a certain path, who listen to what you say. It doesn't go any further than that. In the Whole-World, writers try out their pens and their wings in individual ways; there is no systematic thought, no ideology. If there were systematic thoughts and ideologies, it would mean that we had gone back to the bad old ways and in that case we should not attach much importance to this phenomenon of schools. That writers meet each other, that their poetics touch each other, that their poetics help each other – this is a precious thing, but I don't think we should attach any importance to schools …

L.G. It's a manifestation of solidarity?

É.G. Yes. Solidary and solitary.

L.G. The Writers' Parliament is a manifestation of this solidarity. Do we need to have a new mobilization of writers? Must writers start once again to make themselves heard in the public arena today, because it seems to me that there has been a sort of erasure of the writer's voice?

É.G. What is happening is that today we realize that we rely more and more, alongside politics and economics, on imaginations, on poetics, and even a little on utopias, as long as they are not systematic ideologies. All the world's cultures increasingly rely on two dimensions. The first is the flat literalness deployed by television, radio and newspapers, that is, the illusion that we know the world because there is a levelling out, because we know what has happened on the other side of the world, through the media. And there is another kind of approach to the world which is, let's say, the real imagination of the world-totality. It is this real imagination of the world-totality that counterbalances the media's illusion of real knowledge of the world. That is why writers are once again beginning to have a certain powerful presence in the world-totality, which they all share with each other, in extremely different ways. That is why the idea of a parliament that is in no way ideological and in no way systematic could be interesting. At the same time, many writers in the world can tell themselves: 'If artists who are recognized on the international scene are standing beside me, in a parliament for example, I will be a little more protected in my personal confrontation with my authorities, my public opinion, etc.' This idea of a parliament, which is a great idea from the point of view of imagination, is also a good idea from this point of view: breaking through the isolation of writers in their crucial place and seeking to offer them a sort of rhizome of solidarity in the Whole-World.

L.G. But is there room to hear the writer in present-day societies?

É.G. I believe so. It's true that literature has declined with the appearance of media splashes, but we will go back to it. Just as we are going back to the idea that we must somehow clean up the planet, we will come to this idea that we must take account of the voices of writers. That does not endow them with any particular status, any functional advantage, but it creates for them, as one says, new duties that are, and are only, to do with literature.

NOTE ON THE TEXT

This text meets, crosses, revises (and sometimes just repeats) statements made on the following occasions:

- The Assises Internationales de la traduction, Arles, 1994;
- the conference 'Sociétés et littératures antillaises', University of Perpignan, 1994;
- the 'Journées antillaises' at the universities of Bologna and Parma, 1991;
- the editing of the book *Faulkner, Mississippi*, 1995.

◆ 7 ◆

Watching Out for the World*

Lise Gauvin. *Le monde incréé* has the subtitle 'poétrie'. It contains a mixture of genres but above all drama. Three plays written at different times, that the author states are 'unstageable'. To what does this word 'poétrie' refer?

Édouard Glissant. It's an ambiguous word because it is a French word, 'poétrie', that refers to an English word, poetry. So there is a deliberate intention to confuse, or rather to mix up the origin, a deliberate intention to show that it is not a distinct literary genre, but a mixture of narrative, of stage dialogue, of poetry, of thought, etc. It's the first step towards what could be a 'de-structuring' of genres. Traditional genres such as the novel, drama, the essay. I expect that I will write more and more of this kind of 'poétrie'.

L.G. But doesn't each work have its own form?

É.G. Yes, each work has its own 'poétrie'. But one gets to a point where one has to bring all this together and give it new perspectives, formal perspectives. This is a first attempt to establish those perspectives.

L.G. It is still closer to drama, even though the first play is called 'folktale', the second 'parable', and the third is almost a narrative. Is there perhaps from the start some complicity between drama and history, since these plays refer to particular moments of History? Is drama destined, more than the other genres, to represent History?

---

* Interview with Lise Gauvin, Saint Claude, Guadeloupe, 12 December 2000.

É.G. Not to represent History but to give a deferred image of it. Not a clear image, not an obvious image. Drama, like poetry, is capable of showing things differently. The three plays follow a movement in history, it's true. The first one takes place in an African country, which is not clearly identified, at the moment when colonization and Atlantic slavery are about to begin. The second takes place at the moment when the land is being cleared: it's a sort of parable of the economic history of the country. The third is more specifically concerned with a character who is very dear to me, Marie Celat, or Mycéa, at the moment when she enters into madness. But why does she enter into madness? Because she has an intuitive, obscure knowledge of what happened in the old country, Africa, of what happened in the first play, and she is quite violently affected by the repercussions of this. Amidst the general indifference, she alone has the capacity to go back in time. In other words, the three plays make up a historical sequence – the third being contemporary, around 1985 – but a sequence that is not linear. This enables us to recapitulate to some extent the impossibilities of Antillean history.

L.G. At one point in the text, the 'uncreated world' is described as 'a promise that floated in nothingness'. Doesn't the actual title, *Le monde incréé*, refer to a retrospective view of History associated with a negative judgement? As if to say: 'The world is old but still uncreated'.

É.G. No, not at all. The title, which is not explained in the book except in an indirect way as in the sentence you have quoted, signifies that this is a world that does not proceed from a genesis, does not proceed from a creation of the world. It is a world that proceeds from historical events, i.e. colonization and Atlantic slavery, and which therefore does not give rise to theologies of territory, theologies of belonging, theologies of ancestry, but opens onto an infinite number of possibilities. The uncreated world is the non-theological world, the non-ethnic world. It is the composite world. In my opinion, it is one of the characteristics of the societies of the Americas. Taken together, the three plays try to show that this world has its own sacredness, which is not the sacredness of Genesis, but that of what I call digenesis ['digénèse'], in other words a conjunction of histories that at some point meet up with each other.

L.G. The uncreated world, then, is also a world 'to be created' …

É.G. It is a world to be created but one which is already here, and of which we do not yet have, let's say, an evident knowledge. Therefore, it is a world that one can access only through the powers of imagination and poetic intuition.

L.G. In this uncreated world, one word recurs quite frequently – the word 'country'. We read: 'We are in the other of the country, which must be named'. There are also references to a country 'being cleared', an 'unploughed' country, a country 'more than absent, obscure'. What is the significance of this notion of country, as it appears in the plays?

É.G. The country is the place. The place from which the word comes. I have said in several of my books, including the *Traité du Tout-monde*, that place is crucial, that the word does not come to exist in an abstraction, in an abstract elevation. The word is linked to one landscape, one time, but it tries to meet all the landscapes and all the times of the world. That is what gives it its unenclosed, perpetually open character. The country I am talking about is not a country that imposes itself as a closed reality, sectarian and shut in on itself.

L.G. So this notion of country does not correspond to a political entity.

É.G. No, not at all. It is a poetic entity. Politics is not concerned with these considerations, but politics can sanction an enclosure or politics can try to open onto something. Enclosure or openness, in my view, are not connected to a political movement but are connected to a movement of the imagination of a community.

L.G. As regards history, the play that is about colonization is very ironic, but at the same time very cynical, because we go from an uncultivated country, called Eden, to a country of superstores and consumption, after the period of factories and industrialization. We read this: 'Sheltered from the century and its miseries/ We celebrate we vote'. How do you situate yourself in relation to the idea of postcolonialism, which is very fashionable today?

É.G. I don't feel that I am a postcolonialist, because I am in a history that never stops. The history of the Caribbean is not a frozen history. There is no postcolonial period in the history of the Caribbean, or even the Americas. There is a discontinuum that still weighs on us. If one defines postcolonialism as the fact of being in a period in which one can reflect back on a past phenomenon called colonialism, I say that it's not true. We are still in a colonialist period, but it is a colonialism that has taken a different form. It is colonialism through the domination of the big multinationals. A colonizing country no longer needs to occupy another country in order to colonize it. There is something over-generalizing, synthetic and conclusive in the term 'postcolonialism' that I object to. I consider myself as belonging to a country that is still struggling in the uncertainties of the appropriation of its own values and its own riches. What happens in *Le monde incréé*, that trajectory, that journey from the old country to the kinds of cultivation and occupation of the country, and then to the appearance of elementary forms of madness and suffering, all this seems to me to share the same perspective, which means that I am not at all a postcolonialist.

L.G. In one of the plays they make fun of 'beheaded' words such as 'similation', 'centralization', 'gionalization'. One could add 'globalization'. Is there a way out for smaller communities in this globalized world?

É.G. Yes, but it's not in the nature of a book like this to suggest or propose ways out. The aim of the book is to highlight or suggest the contradictions, the impossibilities, the confusions, the obscurities that result from this historical circuit, and not to propose solutions. The role of poetry, of 'poétrie', is to unearth the questions and obscurities and bring them back up to the surface. The question of whether there is a solution for small countries belongs to a more conceptually organized kind of thought.

My own answer is yes. There are solutions. Fifty years ago, I think, I wrote that within the phenomena of globalization there are fixed points of resistance that are not points of enclosure but are points of participation in the world. This is what I call archipelagic thought. This archipelagic thought is able, for a given community, to assemble the elements that allow it to exist within globalization. The rest belongs to economics, to political science, etc. *Le monde incréé* does not aim to provide solutions but to raise a problem.

L.G. I want now to turn more to your essays. Here you have made considerable use of the idea of the rhizome, taken from Deleuze, but you have never used the concept of minor literature, which was promoted by Deleuze and Guattari in their book on Kafka and has since been taken up by many other people.

É.G. This is a concept that seems to me interesting within the frame of reference in which it has been defined. When one is inside, in the belly of the beast, as Kafka was, or as Deleuze and Guattari were, one can indeed put forward the idea of a minor literature, which triumphantly opposes, as its antithesis, ideas of literatures that are, let's say, 'major'. But we who are in the world consider that our literatures are not minor, nor undervalued, because they are in direct contact with the impulses of the world and we don't have to set up this kind of relation that is internal to Western cultures. As a result, I don't myself make use of the ideas of minor literatures and undervalued literatures as Deleuze and Guattari have defined them.

L.G. In the plays, one notices a play on languages, a mixture of idioms. One even reads a commentary indicating that the author likes this opacity. He even goes so far as to make fun of Shakespeare by comically misspelling his name. Is this way of openly playing with languages confined to drama, in your view?

É.G. The theatre is the place of revelation par excellence. What I call tragic revelation. In dramatic form this revelation is more explicit, more total. In poetry and the novel, but especially in poetry, in my poems, the play on words, the 'interlanguage', is total but not openly advertised. I can give examples of poems where the conflagration of languages is total, where there are inventions of words, of terms, but the actual operation is not advertised as such. Whereas in dramatic form, it proclaims itself, and so appears more obvious.

L.G. In these plays there is also a variation on the figure of the poet. In the first play we have an educated multilingual tramp and, in the last one, a delirious speaker ['déparleur'], who is in a way contrasted with the singers and the 'great namers'. What exactly does the delirious speaker represent?

É.G. The colonial journey that we have followed or that these communities have been made to follow means that poetry, which emanates directly from the substratum of a community, does not appear as such. It takes many detours, the detours of the storyteller, for instance. The delirious speaker is someone who manifests this presence of poetry linked with the impossibility of poetry, which is what is most lacking for us in our countries. There are many novelists, but there is no poetics. This poetics is there. We must go in search of it. The delirious speaker is searching for it, but since he does not have a system of fixed references that would allow him to be a poet and to express the community like Homer or a *chanson de geste* could do, he speaks deliriously. Just as Marie Celat, since she cannot explain why she feels all the impossibilities of the country, goes mad. To speak deliriously is to speak poetry without having the means to formalize it. That seems to me one of the conditions of our countries. The people who don't feel it, write novels.

L.G. To what extent does the delirious speaker contrast with those whom you call 'the great namers'?

É.G. I call 'great namers' those who desperately try to recover the same ancestral root as the delirious speaker, but who are less lucid. The delirious speaker is willing to enter into a fragmented *langage*, apparently empty of meaning, apparently contradictory, apparently far-fetched, whereas the great namer tries to return to the ancestral root, patiently, to show that there is an ancestral root, that there is this and that, that there is a being, etc.

The great namer is the delirious speaker with a kind of naivety that supports him, that protects him. He sings more completely but he does not perceive the drama of the uprooting of the word that the delirious speaker perceives.

L.G. And the singers?

É.G. The singers represent everyday life. Life as it tries to develop outside any consciousness of what has happened.

L.G. So the delirious speaker is another manifestation of the tramp who appears in the first text?

É.G. Absolutely. The delirious speaker is the traditional *driveur*. He is the man who stands at the crossroads deliriously shouting, the man who spectacularly takes upon himself the imbalances of society. He is a new kind of griot. The griot took upon himself the figures of society but in a rhythm, an order and a ceremony which were linked to the African societies. The delirious speaker takes upon himself the disorder of society, but he has become more alone, more solitary, at the crossroads. In order to decipher his words, one needs an obscure awareness of this trajectory that a book like *Le monde incréé* tries to follow.

L.G. The delirious speaker is even able to make fun of his own speech. At one point, he adopts the tone of a pompous poet. He makes 'great poetry'.

É.G. Of course.

L.G. The final play is devoted to Marie Celat, who is presented as 'the woman with the open face'. Is she a kind of Pythia or Cassandra?

É.G. She is all of that. She is also the slave woman who kills her child so that he will not be a slave. She is also the woman who tries to revive the failing collective memory. And she is also the woman who is the victim of men in Antillean society and who nevertheless takes upon herself the movements of this society.

L.G. Can the world of the twenty-first century be as threatening as that of the twentieth century? What is the future of literature today?

É.G. In any case, literature is threatened with disappearance, by the very fact that it is multiplying and increasing so prodigiously. It is literally becoming an image of the confusion, the inexplicability and the unpredictability of the world. As a result, it is relentlessly becoming banal. All consumable literature today is banal literature. That is obvious. That is why this kind of literature consists essentially of novels. Because people believe that the novel is easier, that it can more easily provide the keys to this kind of generalized dereliction. It may happen that literature as a genre disappears. It may also happen that it retreats into obscurities, secrets and depths from which it will reappear later on with the full panoply of modern techniques. It may happen that a new form will appear. We have no way of knowing. We must realize that literature has become a generalized object of production and consumption and that, as a result, it often fails in its purpose, which is to bring up to the surface information, truths and structures that no-one usually sees. It becomes a superficial object, whereas literature has traditionally been an object of depth.

L.G. A final question on these plays: why did you feel the need to write that they are 'unstageable'?

É.G. That's connected to what I have just been saying. A play – but they are not really plays – a literary object that tries to go into the depths cannot really be an object on a stage. Because the stage is the place where depth becomes apparent. But when the depth is inextricable, perhaps this function of making it apparent becomes more difficult and perhaps the play is more unstageable …

Rethinking Utopia*

Lise Gauvin. Édouard Glissant, you have just published an essay, *La Cohée du Lamentin*, subtitled 'Poétique V'. The impression I had from reading you is that it is difficult to distinguish the essayist's prose from that of the poet. Would you say that every essay has a poetic quality, that the two genres can interpenetrate?

Édouard Glissant. The essay has something of poetic writing when it is a tool of discovery, when its purpose is to delve into a subject. Some essays are content to be recapitulations. In that case, the essay can have a rational *langage*, completely organized, structured, clear. But when the essay has as its aim to delve into poetic subject matter, as is the case for *La Cohée du Lamentin*, the style can certainly not be the 'style' of an essay: it must be a poetic style.

L.G. Could one not subtitle this work 'a poetics of place' or perhaps 'the imagination of place'?

E.G. The basic idea is that starting from a particular point that is the Cohée du Lamentin, i.e. one corner of the bay of Lamentin, in a small country, Martinique, in a small archipelago, the Caribbean, one enters into contact with the problems, the difficulties and the hopes of a reality that I call the Whole-World, and that there is therefore an understanding between such a small, unimportant place and the horizons of the Whole-World. That is the central idea of the book, which of course also engages with other areas such as painting, poetry and poetics.

---

* Interview given in March 2005 in Paris. Published in *Francofonia*, no. 50, spring 2007, pp. 115-123.

L.G. The Cohée du Lamentin is the name of a place that really exists but you also say in the book that it is a word whose origin remains a mystery.

É.G. That seemed to me the appropriate designation for this book. The word 'cohée' does not exist in French dictionaries. It doesn't exist in Creole dictionaries. And yet it exists. One can say 'un' or 'une' *cohée*, it doesn't matter which. There is 'la Cohée du Lamentin', 'un fonds Cohée' in Saint-Pierre in Martinique. There is 'une cohée de Basse-Terre'. Therefore, it is a word that varies and resists, which seems to me the very characteristic of any poetics in the world today.

L.G. There is an opacity in the word …

É.G. Yes, it's a word that resists.

L.G. Another word which recurs quite often in this work is the word 'utopia', which you define as 'what we lack in the world'. But you imply that there are two kinds of utopia, that is, utopia as a system of thought and the utopia that is situated on the side of imagination. Could you explain this opposition?

É.G. From the traditional point of view, if we think of Plato's *Republic* or St Augustine's *The City of God*, or More's *Utopia*, utopia is a normative system which acts to confer excellence on an object, whether this be human nature, or the City, or society. As a result, all classic utopias contain an idea of measure, of normality, of excellence and of what works best. It's a sort of desire for eternity, utopian thought. What I am saying is that in our world today, which is a world of diversity, a world of opposites, of contrasts, utopia cannot consist of choosing one of the elements of this diversity or these oppositions and then perfecting it, turning it into an object that no longer changes, that lives in excellence. Utopia for us today means bringing together, with no exceptions, all the beauties, all the suffering and all the values of the world. Therefore, in this accumulation, what will predominate is the feeling and the reality of a Relation between what has been accumulated. Utopia will be a keen sense of a poetics of Relation, whereas, in the traditional sense, utopia is a poetics of excellence and normality. I don't know if that is clear?

L.G. I think so. The traditional utopia presupposes a system that is perfect, and so closed, not in the process of becoming.

É.G. That's right. Whereas utopia, for us, is what is lacking, in other words what allows us to go on accumulating until we reach the whole quantity of elements that make up the Whole-World. So that we try to make sure that none is lacking. Myself, for example, I say that as regards *langage*, if one of the world's languages dies, a part of the human imagination dies. We must struggle against the disappearance of languages, even the tiniest of them, even if they are only spoken by ten people, because they are a representation of the imagination of men and of human communities.

L.G. You criticize everything that seems to you systematic thought, but it seems to me that your own thought relies on oppositions such as: Whole-World/globalization, continental thought/archipelagic thought, structure/process. Don't these oppositions already represent the beginning of a system?

É.G. It's not the system that needs to be criticized: it's the fact that the system is systematic. That is what needs to be criticized. One can have non-systematic systems. One can have chaotic systems. One can have erratic systems. One can have systems with variable dimensions. These systems are no longer systematic. Systematic thinking or systems of thought are those that obey systematic laws. So it is not the notion of system that needs to be criticized, it's the idea that the system forces you to move along a single route, to progress along a single route, forces you into linearities that no longer correspond to the present situation of the world and its chaotic organization.

L.G. Some people might see a contradiction between what you say about the need to act in 'the inextricable reality of the world, without reducing it to [one's] own impulses or individual or collective interests' (p.24) and what you also say about the need to save 'wounded identities'. You write: 'I believe in the future of small countries' (p. 27). How do you articulate these two projects together?

É.G. I have answered this in many of my earlier books. I have tried to explain that the encounter, hybridity and creolization do not aim to end up as a sort of soup, a sort of meaningless melting pot, which would be a mash or a mush of all identities and all places, but that there is a need to define place and identity and then immediately afterwards a need to open them up, that is, to go beyond definitions. Therefore, that's what one says when one says that there is an interdependence. It doesn't mean that everything is mixed up. It means that independences must exist and that these independences consent to interrelations. There is at the start something that is not undifferentiated and there is at the finish something that is not undifferentiated because the totality of these relations is governed by what I call a 'poetics of Relation'; it is not a system but a permanent opening onto as many extensions and relations as possible.

L.G. You have just mentioned creolization, which is one of the key concepts of your poetics. As an example of creolization, you often cite jazz, American jazz. Isn't creolization first and foremost a cultural process? Do you not think that, up to a point, it escapes politics and economics, since these domains are governed by laws that are more rectilinear, more coercive? You don't hesitate to state that 'the cultural imagination becomes a factor' (p. 159). But can the cultural imagination really abolish certain notions, like that of empire, for example? How do you articulate this idea of creolization together with politics and economics?

É.G. As far as the facts are concerned, creolization plays a part in both politics and economics. But creolization has no morality. These are phenomena that exist in reality, phenomena of mixing, hybridity producing unexpected results, that exist in the history of humanity. They took place across infinite expanses of time in the past, which meant that we did not have time to perceive them. Now they take place at prodigious speed, which means that we have the time to become aware of them. The phenomena of civilization happen at such a prodigious speed that it makes us dizzy, we are so to speak stunned.

Creolizations have always existed but have no morality. It is not their role to lead us towards a more compassionate, more law-abiding, less barbarous humanity. What happens is that creolization, which has always existed, has always been rejected by those who believe in the single root-identity. What is happening today is that the phenomena of creolization are beginning to break down these rigidities of the single root-identity. Wherever there have been creolizations in the contemporary world – I'm thinking of places like Beirut or Sarajevo – wherever in the world there have been concrete incidences of creolization, the supporters of single root-identity have been determined to try to destroy them. Creolization is an issue in economics and politics. But, creolization is not a panacea. It is not the means of solving political and economic problems. What I think is that if the phenomena of creolization play a role in the history of human communities, it is to change the orientations of the imaginations of man, of human communities. If we succeed in orientating the imaginations of human communities differently we can find solutions to political and economic problems, solutions that are far more fundamental, permanent and durable than military occupations or global economic decisions. If you take two communities that are fighting in the name of a single root and you put an army in between them, they will of course stop fighting. But as soon as that army leaves, they will start fighting again in the name of the same principles. But if you can make more and more effective the maxim that I can change through exchange with the other without losing or distorting myself, perhaps at that point you will be able to work on the matter of oppositions between single roots and you will be able to get both sides to lay down their arms. This is what I call utopia and what I call the action of poetic thinking on the world. I think that poetic thinking today has as much chance of succeeding as political thinking.

L.G. In this new essay, there is a search for form which produces, notably, passages where one sees 'excipits' appear, summaries of earlier thoughts, conclusions or quotations from your own works. We recognize them as leitmotivs of your thought. I feel that you could have added this one: 'It is given to all languages to build the tower'. This sentence has often been quoted although, in a way, it remains enigmatic. Could you comment on it?

É.G. The idea behind the myth of the tower of Babel is that if each of the workers on the tower speaks a different language the work cannot be co-ordinated and the tower will collapse because it has no unitary principle. In other words, the idea behind the myth of the tower of Babel is that in order to work together one must have a single language. This idea is current in the present-day situation of the world when people say: 'Anglo-American should be the universal language'. Others say that we must create a universal language such as Esperanto. I say no. The development of the Tout-monde is not linked to a single language, whether this is a dominant language or an artificially constructed one. The development of the Tout-monde is linked to the multiplicity of languages. This multiplicity is not an obstacle to understanding between speakers.

I say that for example, more and more, people can listen to poems in foreign languages and be moved by them without understanding the language in which the poem was written. I say that there is a new sensibility developing in human communities and that the relations between one language and another will consist more of intuition and common sense – that is, shared sense – than of intellectual traditions and clear meaning. In other words, there is a certain opacity – I am still in the domain of opacity – in the contact with languages which is not a fault but the acquisition of new abilities in the men and women of today.

L.G. In this essay we also find several expressions of admiration for painters, poets or philosophers. In particular you mention Deleuze, Tabucchi, and Gaston Miron. How would you describe Miron, whom you knew so well?

É.G. I would describe him as a natural phenomenon, as a sort of eruption, but also as a sort of calm emergence, abundant and rhythmical, who lived his expansion in space with passion. That is why I say he is a natural phenomenon.

L.G. You also talk about Césaire, the poet. Don't you think that the tensions between certain generations of Antillean writers and Césaire have been exaggerated? Has Césaire's trajectory as a militant or a politician perhaps cast a shadow over the poet? It seems to me that in your work there is a desire to rediscover the words of the poet.

É.G. I don't need to rediscover him. I never lost him. Since I started teaching, I have regularly devoted part of my teaching to Césaire's poetry. So I have never lost Césaire's poetry. His political positions have certainly got in the way of perception of the real qualities of his writing. For myself, I have always regretted the way in which his poetry has been reduced to a kind of declaration of principles revolving around Negritude. But that is not all it is. There is the fundamental quality of a great poet, whether he promotes Negritude or not. It is possible, now that Césaire's political life has more or less come to an end, that people can be more open to the poetry itself. As far as I am concerned, I have never lost sight of it!

L.G. You have a rather remarkable definition of poetry. You write: 'Poetry does not produce the universal, no, it gives birth to upheavals that change us'.

É.G. That is what I believe.

L.G. Throughout the essay, there is the desire to draw up an inventory of human suffering. You cite for instance news bulletins that are all very alarmist. You name the cataclysms that are happening everywhere on the planet, but at the same time there is the desire to resist apocalyptic thinking. Would you say that what you are proposing is a new humanism?

É.G. I would not say that it is a new humanism because the very notion of humanism has something of a system of thought that I do not like: I would say that it is perhaps a new approach to human communities, as they are lived today in the contemporary world, but not a new humanism. I don't claim to arrive at humanism because, whatever anyone says, there is in the idea of humanism once again a moral dimension that seems to me unnecessary.

L.G. Your thought remains quite optimistic …

É.G. I am resolutely optimistic but that does not mean that I am founding a new system of humanism. Optimism means trusting in the effectiveness of interrelations between many systems: systems of cultures, of languages, of landscapes, of countries. It's not a humanism, it's a poetics.

L.G. What is the role of the writer or the intellectual today?

É.G. I cannot say if the writer, the intellectual, has a role, but I can say that there is a role for poetry and art. This role, which I try to track in my books, is linked to what I am always saying: we must change the imaginations of human communities. I believe that only poetry and art are the decisive driving forces here.

9

On Beauty as Complicity*

Lise Gauvin. If one tries to summarize this book, *Une nouvelle région du monde*, would it be right to say that it is the result of vertigo and trembling in the face of the beauty of the world?

Édouard Glissant. I don't know if it's a result, but it is part of a fairly dizzying vision of the world and the beauty of the world. That is true. Is it vertigo? Perhaps it's also something else.

L.G. Isn't the idea of beauty, which recurs like a leitmotiv in the book, a certain kind of transcendence? Isn't it a kind of tension towards being? Something that participates in Being with a capital B?

É.G. Not at all. At least not in my conception of beauty. In fact it's the opposite. I start from the idea that beauty, which may or may not be perceived, can be the signal of a meeting in difference of created objects and of natural things. It is the signal that one difference is inviting and approaching differences that affix themselves to the first one and form a density that can be trembling, not fully achieved, but that has nothing to do with transcendence.

L.G. What is the connection with the *Traité du Tout-monde*, which you designate as a 'Poetics'?

É.G. The connection is obvious because it is a vision of the world, of what I call the Whole-World, which is not a part of the world but a region of the world into which we all enter at the same time. That is what makes it new.

---

* This interview took place in Paris on 17 October 2006.

The difference is that this book is about the work of beauty whereas the *Traité du Tout-monde* was about how to approach the diversity of the world. That work was not specifically about the beauty of the world.

L.G. What is the new region exactly and what is its relationship to the whole?

É.G. The region is new because it is the region that some of us have already entered, Rimbaud and many other individuals, but it is a region that we are now called upon to enter all together. That is what makes it new. It is a new region of the world because we live in the world, the world is there in front of us, inside us or beside us, but we have not yet understood that there is a part of the world that we see or we don't see, into which we must all enter together, that is, in which we must put our differences into relation without these differences leading to disasters. These differences in us and for us indicate the beauty of the world. That is why there is a Whole-World, a new region of the world, beside the world itself, in the world itself, beyond the world itself, this side of the world itself, and indistinguishable from the world itself.

L.G. You say that we are going to enter a new region of the world, but you reject the idea of the end of an era. You write: 'We are all young in the Whole-World'. Is there an evolution in the world? If so, what kind of evolution? Is there a passage of time?

É.G. I don't think there is an evolution, because I believe that the world is unforeseeable and unpredictable. Evolution is characteristic of a reality, a logical entity, that is harmonious and sequential. Our connection to the world and the world itself are unforeseeable, unpredictable. I don't believe that anything in this domain is consequential. It is possible that the end of the world is there, in a manner that may be climatological, or geological, or thermal … it is possible, but it's not something that should constitute an obsession for the human imagination. What should constitute an obsession for the human imagination, and what the human imagination should learn to come to terms with, is the idea that the beauty of the world comes about through the differences between these realities. It is this idea that we have not yet explored or revealed. That is why the differences in the world lead to so many catastrophes, so many untenable positions. When we look at our differences with the rest of the world, we become intolerant, fundamentalist in relation to ourselves and to our beliefs. In that sense, this book is also a eulogy of difference. Difference is not what separates us. It is the elementary particle of all relation. It is on the basis of difference that what I call Relation with a capital R functions.

L.G. You write that the realized quantity of all the differences in the world leads you to accept the idea of the universal. It's a word that recurs several times in the text. And yet, we know your distrust of this word and the implicit assumptions on which it is based.

É.G. If we say that, we must immediately add that what I am prepared to envisage as a universal is the *realized* quantity of all the differences and that alone. I do not claim that this realized quantity ends up as a sort of unity that would abolish the particularity of each of the differences. And as a result, this realized quantity is the opposite of a certain kind of universal. This universal is the ideal that is *realizable* on the basis of several real phenomena.

What I am defending is the idea that beauty comes about as the result of a gradually realized quantity.

The ideal contained in the notion of the universal disappears in the notion of realized quantity.

L.G. You use the pronoun 'we', you say 'we all'. What does this 'we' cover, exactly?

É.G. It is made up of so many different instances of 'we' – opposed, contradictory, mutually hostile – that, paradoxically, it is a 'we' that is an unrealized quantity. Some instances are communitarian, some identitarian, some associative. There are also some that would consent to the work of difference. These instances of 'we' are not yet realized. They must be realized in order for all of us to enter this new region of the world.

L.G. Do you think that this new region of the world will be realized one day? That would presuppose the end of fundamentalisms, of sectarianisms …

É.G. I do think so. This doesn't mean that it would signify the end of particularisms. The 'we' is not the end of differences, of disagreements. But it would be the end of the imposition of disagreements on an essential level, which would be the level of the acceptance of the other.

L.G. Let's come back to works of art. You talk about the beauty of prehistoric works, saying that it is inexplicable, and that 'the same and the other were not experienced as separate'. You talk about an art of 'magnetic connection' which has been followed by 'a utilitarian art'. Is this a point of no return?

É.G. Not at all. I think that in the history of all arts and all cultures there is a nostalgia for this primordial – not primitive – moment when the same existed in relation to the other. The 'same' who was the cave-dweller, for instance, his other was not other people; it was the animals and the surroundings. In this sense, when he encounters other people and the wars start, and social life starts, he abandons the attempt at fusion and communion with the other in the form of the animals and the surroundings, to enter into the vicissitudes of life in society and perhaps in history. That is to say, the relation with another person, an other that is similar to himself. It seems to me that the whole history of the arts of all human communities is a kind of tension towards this point of fusion, of complicity with the other that is an animal, or a tree, or the other of things, and that this obscure tension has always been – perhaps fortunately because it is an unbearable tension – masked, blocked, by a conception of beauty as obeying rules, obeying laws, complying with a prescription.

There is this duality in how we think of beauty. Once again, I go back to Rimbaud. When he says 'One must become a seer', he is saying that one must be capable of seeing this moment of primordial fusion. And I think that people have tried, through the regulation of the beautiful, to forget this moment. Perhaps we are coming back to it now because it seems to me to be more and more evident, because the purely social and historical relation, i.e. the relation between communities, has reached an incredible paroxysm.

And also because the relation to the other of nature, the other of the tree, the other of the forest has reached a point of unbearable vacillation and imbalance.

We are victims at one and the same time of wars and social intolerance, and of natural disasters – earthquakes, fires, tidal waves, tsunamis, etc.

For the first time perhaps, there are two opposing masses, and that makes us pay attention to their real connections. That is why there is something happening at this time. It makes human sensibility more acute, and perhaps it also helps us to perceive more clearly the nature of the beauty of the world.

L.G. You make a distinction between beauty, which is always variable, and the beautiful, which presupposes a certain number of rules. Does the beautiful exist outside subjectivity? Doesn't the notion of the beautiful presuppose a gaze, a judgement?

É.G. The notion of the beautiful presupposes that within us there still exist traces of that primordial relation that I have spoken about, and that attempt at fusion and complicity with an other that is not other people but the environment, i.e. nature, animals. There is still the nostalgia for this, but now it is framed by the social rules of construction that man gives himself. The beautiful is a social product. Beauty is an aspiration for everyone. That is the big difference. One does not aspire to the beautiful, but one understands it and constructs it. Aesthetics in the traditional sense is the science of that construction. But aesthetics for me is the intuition of that relation of complicity that I have been talking about.

L.G. What do you understand by 'utilitarian art'?

É.G. The art that serves to assert the singularity, the exceptional nature of a given community. An art that excludes any participation by another community. It can be religious art. It is not a hybrid art, an art of fusion and mixing. It is an art of singularity for a given community. It is a social art. It is an art that facilitates social relations within a single community. This can be very good. But it is not an art of intuition, it is not an art that trembles. It is an art that obeys rules and laws that are quite fixed, an art that has quite precise views, since everyone is convinced that the community within which they live is the best one, and they cannot tolerate any others.

L.G. Apart from religious art, are there any other examples?

É.G. The art of representing totems can be a religious art but it can also be quite simply an art that represents a community. The totem is a utilitarian art because it is an art that brings together the emblems of a bird, or some other animal. If there is an animal which emblematically represents the strength of a community, it is represented in an idealized fashion.

L.G. It's an art that has a determinate function.

É.G. Of course.

L.G. How do you situate so-called primitive or 'first' arts in this very general history of art?

É.G. The arts that are first, primitive, indigenous, remote, or whatever, are those that have not had a function in the world because they have remained on the level of complicity with the other, but not as other people, rather the other as environment or as animal. They are arts that have participated in the search for this complicity. Secondly, they are arts that have had no influence in the world, except when they have been 'discovered', when some artists from the conquering civilizations have been inspired by them, as though they were attempts that have been preserved solely for the moment when the kind of encounters that we experience today can take place. Unfortunately, when these encounters have taken place, it has been in the context of such injustice, such imbalance in the conditions of existence, that in fact it just delays even further the moment when, in spite of the imitations by Picasso, Braque or others of African art, we could gain a new overall vision of these different artistic procedures: the social art representative of the Western civilizations, and the art that is an obscure, tentative memory of the complicity of civilizations such as the African ones. This synthesis cannot yet be achieved in our imagination because there is such a difference in the real conditions of these various groups that as yet no-one can see that such a synthesis might be possible. But we must see it if we want to enter the new region of the world.

L.G. All these works of art have been moved, taken away to the centres. We can discover them thanks to museums, but at the same time they are deprived of their natural setting.

É.G. That's why it is difficult to imagine what might result from these encounters that are happening now. A new aesthetic is an aesthetic which tries to predict, presage, or see these encounters in the future.

L.G. Once again you address the difference between language and *langage*. You say: 'The language sometimes disappears but the *langage* that supports a work of art persists and lasts'. Or, again: 'Languages establish, *langages* situate'. You seem to believe that *langages*, works of art, last longer than languages.

É.G. It's a common place. Latin has disappeared but we still read the *Aeneid*. We read it in translation but one can also read it in the original. And every literary work is a *langage* in relation to the language in which it is expressed.

Langage is language, but, as Deleuze would say, reduced ['minorée'], that is, language used in the perspective of art.

A folk tale spoken in a language is a *langage* in relation to that language, even if that language is only an oral one. That is the distinction I make between the notions of language and *langage*.

L.G. You say that the *langages* of painters, sculptors, architects, musicians and philosophers are of the same kind. But you seem to have a preference for sculptors …

É.G. Not really. I wrote a passage on sculptors and sculpture perhaps because it's the only art that is really common to the diverse zones of artistic expression. There is no painting in the Western sense in Africa. There are no etchings in the oriental sense in the African countries. But the activity of the sculptor is everywhere. It's not a preference, it's a way of saying that it is one of the common places of representation or of the attempt at complicity in the arts of the world.

L.G. As regards languages, you say that languages modify and transform themselves. You talk about the codes of complicity that exist in the suburbs and are part of a form of creolization. But where does creolization end? To what extent can a creolization that is too strong make a language disappear?

É.G. The world is unpredictable. Who can say whether a language is eternal or not? We know today that there are dead languages that continue to live and that others disappear completely. In any case, it's not an interesting question. The accumulation of relations between languages includes many injustices and miracles, and youth and old age. It is always sad when a language dies. If there is only one way of saying 'l'eau', that's a terrible limitation on the human imagination. If everyone says *water*, it is no longer an element of relation between man and the world, but an element of codification. Consequently, we must defend with all our strength the diversity of languages and fight with all our strength against the disappearance of languages. But one cannot make any kind of prediction about this.

L.G. One passage in the book mentions francophony as deriving from the colonizer–colonized relation. Can we think about francophony outside this relation? On the other hand, you say that there is no longer any legitimate centre or periphery but, as regards France, you say that it can become the focus of a universalizing culture. How do you see this question of francophony today?

É.G. It's clear that any attempt at this kind of community can only be a consequence of the colonial enterprise. When a colonizer joins up with some of the colonized, the old colonizer–colonized relation is bound to be an underlying presence. What we must do is not forget this old relation, but make the various memories of it join together and combine. Because forgetting is not a form of reunion. It's not a form of solidarity. But nor is memory for the sake of revenge. The form of solidarity consists of memories that come together to open up a new dimension. It's difficult to do. It doesn't happen from one day to the next. The ex-colonized may still have a reaction of bitterness or else of withdrawal towards the ex-colonizer. Unconsciously, the latter may have a slight reaction of superiority. It is always difficult to establish these relations. Forgetting is not a solution. Because forgetting leaves intact the possible grievances, the possible susceptibilities, the possible feelings of inferiority, the possible feelings of superiority, even if they are slight and unconscious. The only way of solving this kind of thing is through the conjunction of memories that come together. And that's difficult to do. The other difficulty, if one is sketching out this kind of rapprochement and solidarity, is knowing what francophony is doing in the world. Knowing how it functions in relation to other possible collectivities. That's difficult too. A collectivity such as the Commonwealth is very difficult to define. Is it a collectivity, or is it not? Like francophony, it is very difficult to define. What the relationships between the Commonwealth and francophony will be is also very difficult to define. As a result, we must think about these questions in a trembling way, a way of thinking that does not decide once and for all, that does not come down on one side or the other, and does not base itself on principles that would turn into laws. If it is necessary for the life of the world that these kinds of communities exist, then they will exist. If it's not necessary, they will disappear.

L.G. There are some regions of francophony that are not and have never been within the colonizer–colonized relation. I'm thinking of Belgium, Switzerland and, up to a point, of Quebec. Here we are not within the colonizer–colonized relation.

É.G. There are cultural dominations. When Baudelaire says that he doesn't like the Belgians, he doesn't need actual colonization in order to set up a relation that is one of colonization. In the nineteenth century when it was said that a country that speaks several languages is an inferior country, like Switzerland, Belgium, Quebec or Canada, a relation of colonization was established. Colonization as a presence is not needed in order for colonization to exist. Perhaps this relationship is then only all the more insidious and difficult.

◆ 10 ◆

Movements of Languages and Territories of the Novel*

L.G. You once wrote: 'I write in the presence of all the world's languages, even if I do not know them'. After the showing of Nurith Aviv's film, *From one language to the other* (2006), in which we hear several accounts by poets and novelists who have moved through several languages and now write in Hebrew, I'd like to know if in your opinion the fact of speaking or having moved through several languages gives one a particular predisposition towards writing.

É.G. I don't believe that the fact of knowing several languages gives one a particular predisposition towards writing. What does produce such a predisposition is the fact of having a particular predisposition towards one *langage*, whether this *langage* exists in one language or in several languages. There is in my opinion no quantitative measure of a predisposition towards writing in the knowledge of several languages. In the film that we have seen, what was interesting was that there was a generalizing language, i.e. Hebrew, which for a Jewish or Hebrew population existed in more or less subtle contradiction with so-called original or maternal languages, for example German, Arabic or Hungarian. The film shows that a language can be at once maternal and dominant and exclude other languages. For these people Hebrew has become a mother tongue through the belief of the Israelis. It nonetheless continues to be a dominant language for the mother tongues, some of which are terribly scarred, like German. There is here a jumble of facts which get tangled up and sometimes result in situations of resignation. Some of these writers look overwhelmed. They quite clearly do not look excited or happy with their lot. I think it's because these are people who belong to our Western civilizations for which the language is

---

* Interview given in 2009 at Le Diamant, Martinique.

an absolute. In these conditions, Hebrew on the one hand and German on the other, or Hebrew and Hungarian, or Hebrew and Arabic, Hebrew appears as an occupier, the occupier of a territory of the absolute, which was previously occupied by others.

In Martinique the situation is different. The occupier is an absolute – French. The occupied, Creole, is not an absolute. It is a plural, multiple language, which does not have ONE source, ONE belief, ONE development. It seems to me that the tragic, pathetic and perhaps unresolved aspect of the situation of the writers, the artists, the poets and musicians of Aviv's film is a very particular one. It is not the situation of a young African child who naturally speaks four languages: the language of his clan, the language of his tribe, the language of his nation and the dominant language of his region, either English, French or Swahili, since Swahili has become a dominant language. This situation does not lead to the same tragic acceptances of a multilingualism that is not yet resolved. All the more so because these people who started off speaking German or Hungarian or Polish all want to speak Hebrew. They say that they want to speak Hebrew but they also say that they find doing so difficult.

L.G. Since the languages of origin were absolutes, there is therefore a confrontation of different absolutes, with Hebrew having the status of a dominant language. One of the writers says he had to murder his first language in order to master Hebrew. So it is no longer a case, as it is in Africa and elsewhere, of a diglossic relation between languages, but rather a relation of domination, or even the extinction, of a language of origin.

É.G. The problem is that Hebrew as an absolute language replaces other absolute languages: German, Hungarian, Russian, etc. In the situations of black Africa, the dominant languages don't replace absolute languages that already have a thousand years of history. In the film we have seen, people are suffering much more because they speak, they live, they dream in Hebrew, but they also speak, live and dream in Hungarian, in Russian, in German ... This creates a contradiction, a fantastic pathos. One can only overcome this pathos by accepting the idea that there are no absolute languages. It is difficult today for people who are used to absolute languages to say that there no longer are any. The actors in the film all spoke Hebrew but one would think that they all spoke different languages.

L.G. How would you distinguish between Hebrew, which is a dominant language in a particular place, and another dominant language or dominant languages that develop across a wider area?

É.G. There is no difference. The only difference is that the political will behind the Russian language, the German language and the Hungarian language has existed for a long time in the history of Europe, whereas the political will behind the Hebrew language has become apparent very recently, with the creation of the state of Israel. It is the state of Israel that has raised to the political dimension the absolute of the Hebrew language that already existed. It was a religious, incantatory, mystical absolute, whereas now it is also a political absolute. That is what happened with the other languages. But it happened earlier. The political absolute of the French language started with the unification of the French kingdom under Louis XIII and Louis XIV, with Colbert and others. The political absolute of the German language came about much later, with Bismarck. The political absolute of the Italian language came about with Victor-Emmanuel II, king of Italy. Whereas the political absolute of the Hebrew language came about much more recently, with the creation of the state of Israel. That is why there is a time-lag, but this time-lag has been reabsorbed by the unifying action of the Jewish religion.

L.G. From a political point of view, how do you see the evolution of languages in the future? Will some languages dominate?

É.G. Unlike many people, I don't believe in the simplification of languages. It has been tried with Esperanto, but it doesn't work. You can't speak Esperanto in a little town with a church, a mosque or a synagogue … People are not going to speak Anglo-American all over the world. There is a period in which Anglo-American spreads because it has the support of technical forces – cinema, television, IT systems whose *langage* is Anglo-American. But that won't last, because the process in which the world is becoming 'archipelagized' will necessarily have an equivalent on the level of *langages*. And languages will cease to have hierarchies. For me, the French language is precious, even fundamental, but not more important than Hungarian, Polish or Swedish. So there will no longer be a hierarchy of languages. As a result, several phenomena will occur. Firstly, languages will lose their sacred status. They will no longer be linked to religions. A day will come when people who are not Jewish will speak Hebrew. They will learn it because they like the Hebrew language, its sonorities. I am convinced of this because there are a lot of people who learn Chinese or Arabic or Japanese without a religious reason. Simply because of the necessity of Relation in the world. I'm not talking about commercial necessities, but psychic, psychological necessities. We need Relation. There are people who choose, for instance, the Chinese language and who learn it very quickly. Whereas if I try to learn it, it will take me five years, ten years. I will suffer. There are people who learn it in one year. Because, in Relation, they are drawn to that. They have no need to believe in Buddhism, or Mao Tse-tung, etc. Therefore, languages will diversify, multiply and become archipelagic, and I believe that the languages that are lucky enough not to disappear when that situation comes about, will become more beautiful.

L.G. When there is an archipelagization, is there necessarily a creolization of the languages?

É.G. There is a creolization, But, let's be careful, the penetration of languages used to be considered a bad thing. People didn't want there to be French words in the English language, or English words in the French language. Which is an absurdity. Because half the words in the English language come from French after the Norman landings in the Middle Ages. And it's quite normal that there should be English words coming into the French language, because of the influence of American techniques and technologies. That is not creolization. We are wrong to defend ourselves against it. These are the conditions of existence in the modern world. But creolization is something else. It is the entry of the systems of poetic images of one language into another. That is true creolization. It's not a question of words. For example, when Martiniquan schoolboys said: *'Stop seeking'*. *'Seeking'* meant for them 'to badmouth someone' ['faire du sucre']. But that has no meaning in any language. Neither in French nor in English. *To be seeking* means to badmouth someone or to make someone believe something that does not exist. So, it's a poetics. Because it is not a use of words. It's a use of a grammatical form. This grammatical form is applied to a word that they themselves invent. This is a total creolization. You use an English form, *to be seeking*, with a word that comes from nowhere – *seeking* comes from 'sucre' [sugar], 'sik' in Creole – and you create something that is new in any language in the world. That is real creolization. I'm not an admirer of what Chamoiseau says about Monchoachi's explorations of Creole forms. It's when he abandons Creole form per se to use instead something approaching it that poetic creation happens. What is important in creolization is that languages contaminate each other. That is the phenomenon. It's not when they borrow words from one another.

L.G. Nevertheless there are languages that disappear. Are there creolizations that don't succeed?

É.G. If a language disappears, it's never because of creolization. A language disappears because all the people who use it have been killed. It happens all the time in Africa. There are tribes of two hundred, three hundred or four hundred people and they are all killed. Or the language disappears because the culture of that language disappears into the culture of a bigger entity. Languages like Swahili absorb the small cultures that are inside it. For example, Bete will disappear because it is spoken by only six hundred thousand people in the middle of a group where six million people speak Swahili. It is not because of creolization but because of the actual conditions of existence of the language. Why hasn't Creole disappeared yet? Because it exists essentially in islands. If Creole were spoken in a corner of Brittany it would already have disappeared, because it would already have been absorbed in the normal way. I don't know if Breton will disappear. But Breton has a lot of difficulty in surviving, because it is inside an entity that is gradually gnawing away at it. Here, the gnawing away is intellectual, but the Creole language is protected by the conditions of the archipelago. That is why the Creole languages exist almost exclusively in archipelagos. They hardly exist at all in continents. There is no Creole language between Quechua and Spanish. There is no Creole language between the Navajo Indians and English. There is no Creole because it is continental. In continental space, the dominant language envelops. And extinguishes. Whereas in the archipelagic spaces the dominated language can survive. It can survive in caricatural forms. It can survive in diminished forms. But it survives. That's why I think that it is in the archipelagos that the phenomena of creolization are the most interesting to observe.

L.G. Let's leave the question of languages now and move on to the question of the novel. Recently, during a conference at the Sorbonne on 'the nation named novel', you quoted Faulkner who used to say: 'I am a failed poet' and you announced the death of the novel in the contemporary era. You asserted that the novel was an out-dated form that had been overtaken by other genres. I would like you to say more about this conception of the novel as failing to adapt to today's civilization or as no longer relevant in accounting for the real.

É.G. I'm going to reply very schematically, since to treat the question fully I would need a hundred pages, which I shall probably write. What I mean is that in the histories of the peoples of the world, at the moment when communities and nations are created, and written literature appears – I am leaving aside the case of oral literature – it becomes necessary to communicate within the community the history of that community, but as separated from myth, legend and religion. Myth, legend, religion, folk tales can be presented in writing. But a time comes when it is necessary for this to become political. Politics is the history of the city. *Polis* in Greek means 'city'. At this point, narrative appears and in Western societies is gradually transformed into the art of the novel. This process varies according to the groups and the nations. It can take one or two centuries. The first novels really appear in England and France. Afterwards, it goes to Germany and then Italy, etc. This means that the novel is a community's narrative of its constitution as a civil community. The novel is not a religious story, not a legendary story, not a mythical story, it is a political story, in the sense of the organization of the city. When the same Western communities colonized the world, the novel gradually and unconsciously became the art of those who, having conquered the world, have the right to speak of it. The art of those who, having conquered the world, have the right to conquer the narrative of the world.

The Western narrative has mushroomed in this incredible way. The Western novel is not so much a technique – there can be all kinds of techniques – as it is a claim, a belief. It is the belief that you can recount history and the world, that you alone can recount it because you alone control it. That is the fundamental belief. It is a belief shared by the most generous writers, like Balzac, and the sickliest writers, like Proust. That is why the novel became, unconsciously and automatically, the fundamental element of literature. Which it absolutely is not. Every important novel in literature is a poetics, above all a poetics. That is why I think it was brilliant of Faulkner to say 'I am a failed poet'. He meant by that: 'I cannot say what I have to say through the channel of poetry but I will say it through the channel of a poetics that goes beyond all the existing forms of literature'. That is why he has the courage to say 'I am a failed poet'. A mediocre novelist would never have that courage.

L.G. And Joyce?

É.G. Joyce interests me only to the extent that he was interested in de-structuring the Western novel. But what Faulkner does is not a de-structuring of the old Western novels, what he does is enable the emergence of a new literary genre that goes beyond the novel.

L.G. So we are no longer in that era of the novel, since Western societies no longer dominate the world …

É.G. And especially because they are falling apart …

L.G. What is replacing the novel or will replace it?

É.G. If I knew, I could tell you.

L.G. Poetry?

É.G. Poetry has always replaced everything. Poetry has always been the crux of literature. Because poetry is the only literary art which says without saying while still saying. That's what Faulkner did with his books. He says without saying while still saying. That is why he arrived at poetry, that's why he arrived at a poetics which other novelists cannot even envisage.

L.G. So there is no future for narrative, in your view?

É.G. No, none. It's over. Narrative will become a folkloric mode of the existence of literatures. I'm sure of it. Because the future of literatures is the inextricable, the incomprehensible, the obscure and the too vast, the too luminous, the too brilliant … There is excess in the future of literatures, and the novel is the perverted art of making literary and commercial profit.

L.G. You also challenge, in several of your works, the notion of the universal. Is there a universal that is not a dominant universal? You also say that not all cultures need the universal. Is the universal an out-dated category?

É.G. All cultures need Relation. They do not need the universal. The universal is above. The universal tries to bring about order and clarity and the cultures must try to bring about Relation between them. We don't need the universal. The problem is that once the West is no longer dominating the world, we will no longer need narrative either. I will not need a novel to understand Chinese culture. It will be able to come via a prayer, a poem, a song, an evocation, a silence …

But it will always come via a poem.